S0-CAA-181

Jim Wiberg
Pension Committee
VWR Corporation
August, 1987

Pension Funds and the Bottom Line

Managing the Corporate Pension Fund as a Financial Business

ABOUT THE AUTHOR

Keith Ambachtsheer studied economics and finance at the Royal Military College of Canada, the University of Western Ontario, and McGill University. He was an investment analyst with Sun Life Assurance Company from 1969 to 1972 and a partner and research director of Canavest House, a brokerage firm specializing in investment technology services for institutional investors, from 1972 until 1981. From 1981 until late 1984 he was a partner and senior consultant with Pension Finance Associates, a firm offering advisory and information services to pension plan sponsors.

A respected author and commentator on pensions and investment topics, his articles have appeared regularly in the *Financial Analysts Journal,* the *Journal of Portfolio Management,* and other professional journals. He has been a co-winner of the Graham and Dodd Award (1979) and the Roger Murray Award (1983). Both awards are for best papers; the former in the *Financial Analysts Journal,* the latter for the Institute for Quantitative Research in Finance, a U.S.-based organization funded by corporations and institutional investors.

He has contributed chapters to two widely-read investment texts— *The Investment Managers' Handbook,* Dow Jones-Irwin, 1980, and *Managing Investment Portfolios,* Warren, Gorham, & Lamont, 1983. A number of his articles have been included in the Institutional Investor Books series edited by Peter L. Bernstein. Mr. Ambachtsheer is vice-chairman of the Financial Research Foundation of Canada.

The author consults on pension and investment matters to governments, industry associations, pension plan sponsors, and organizations providing services to pension plan sponsors. He lives in Toronto with his wife Virginia and daughters Julie and Jane.

Pension Funds and the Bottom Line

Managing the Corporate Pension Fund as a Financial Business

Keith P. Ambachtsheer

DOW JONES-IRWIN
Homewood, Illinois 60430

To Virginia. . .
and to Julie and Jane. . .

Who in their own special ways
helped transform this book
from idea to reality. . . .

©DOW JONES-IRWIN, 1986

All rights reserved. No part of this publication may be
reproduced, stored in a retrieval system, or transmitted,
in any form or by any means, electronic, mechanical,
photocopying, recording, or otherwise, without the prior
written permission of the publisher.

This publication is designed to provide accurate and
authoritative information in regard to the subject matter
covered. It is sold with the understanding that the
publisher is not engaged in rendering legal, accounting, or
other professional service. If legal advice or other expert
assistance is required, the services of a competent
professional person should be sought.

From a Declaration of Principles jointly adopted by a Committee
of the American Bar Association and a Committee of Publishers.

ISBN 0-87094-708-7

Library of Congress Catalog Card No. 85-72699

Printed in the United States of America

1 2 3 4 5 6 7 8 9 0 K 3 2 1 0 9 8 7 6

North American society is getting older. As a consequence, there will be fewer workers to support each pensioner in the coming decades. If we are to maintain our high standard of living in the face of a rising dependency ratio, we must ensure that the productivity of our labor and capital resources continues to rise.

Pension funds have become extremely important vehicles in converting retirement savings into productive capital and have built up a significant ownership position in that productive capital. Thus these funds will play a pivotal role in determining North American living standards in the coming decades.

Pension funds have also become important in a different way. Employer pension plan assets and liabilities now rival those of the main-line businesses of North American employers in size. Through their rapid growth over the last decade, employer pension plans have transformed the financial characteristics of their sponsors. More and more, the capital structure of a corporation cannot be understood without understanding the capital structure of the corporation's pension system.

Given their importance, surprisingly little has been written about the relationship between pension funds and the enterprises that sponsor them. Nor have the operational implications of that relationship been thoroughly explored. This book is about understanding the relationship and its operational implications. In theme and chapter organization, it is hopefully true to its title: *Pension Funds and the Bottom Line: Managing the Corporate Pension Fund as a Financial Business*. I believe it is the first book to tackle the employer pension plan as an entity that has most if not all of the attributes of a financial division or subsidiary of the corporation.

While the book is written first and foremost for those with direct responsibility for the financial management of the corporate pension plan, it should appeal to a much broader audience. Investment managers, actuaries, accountants, regulators, and legislators all play important roles in the management, administration, and regulation of employer pension plans.

The author also hopes that educators and their students focusing on financial intermediaries in general and the financial management of pension plans in particular will find this book a useful supplement to the more theoretical works in these areas.

Writing a book of this nature requires three fundamental ingredients: ideas, time, and money. Probably the most precious of these three is the first ingredient. Without ideas a book doesn't get very far. While this book has only one author, it could not have been written without the intense collaborative efforts of three individuals over more than a decade.

Bob Mitchell and the author were partners at Canavest House from 1973 to 1978. There, we consulted to investment managers on assignments ranging from organizational design to marketing strategies for their services.

During 1978 the author reviewed most chapters of a book titled *Understanding Pension Fund Finance and Investment.* The book was being written by Don Ezra, a prominent actuary. In many ways this book proceeds from, builds on, and advances ideas first introduced in Ezra's book, published in 1979.

Mitchell, Ezra, and the author worked together as consultants to pension plan sponsors at Pension Finance Associates from 1981 to 1984. It was during this period—in the course of hands-on client assignments, internal debate, research at both the micro and macro levels—that a simple but powerful idea emerged.

The idea was that a defined benefit employer pension plan is conceptually a financial subsidiary of the employer. From this central, integrating idea, a fully developed set of principles and practices for managing corporate pension plans evolved.

Policy questions related to the amount of capital the business should have and how it should be deployed and managed came to be addressed in a logical, commonsense manner. Operational and control questions relating to risk and return from investment operations and how to monitor results were also answered in powerful and sometimes highly unique ways.

As the book examines these areas of pension plan financial management in turn, the author is most pleased to share any credit for insight and solutions with his two former associates. Helpful suggestions from a number of people on how to improve chapter drafts are also gratefully acknowledged. Peter Bernstein, Brendan Calder, Chuck D'Ambrosio, Jim Farrell, Walter Good, Don Ivison, Robert Jeffrey, John Maginn, Roger Murray, Don Reed, Ralph Sultan, and Don Walcot were especially helpful. Any remaining errors and omissions are the author's alone.

There were two ingredients in addition to ideas that I mentioned as important to writing a book. The two—time and money—go hand in hand. Financial support from Beutel, Goodman and Company, Brendan Calder Management, Inc., and The Counsel Trust Company permitted me to spend most of the first four months of this year working on the manuscript that has now become this book. While they probably don't agree with everything I say in the book, I hope they are pleased that they played a material role in its publication.

Keith P. Ambachtsheer

CONTENTS

PART FOUR
Control   137

8. Control: From Information to Judgment   139
Control Systems and Control Systems: *The Pension Balance Sheet: A Focal Point for the Control System. Sources of Change in Value of Pension Liabilities. Sources of Change in Value of the Pension Assets. From Information to Judgment. Capital Market Efficiency, Noise, and Signals.* Monitoring Pension Balance Sheet Changes at ALPHA Corporation: *Putting the Spotlight on Asset Management. From Information to Judgment.* Chapter Notes.

PART FIVE
The Future   153

9. The Private Pension System Challenge: Achieving "Legitimacy"   155
The Private Pension System Under Attack: *The "Legitimacy" Issue. The System 10 Years Later. Pension Reform at ALPHA Corporation.* Chapter Notes.

Index   165

PART ONE

The Pension Fund as a Business

CHAPTER ONE

Understanding the Pension Fund as a Financial Business

The problem of our age is the proper administration of wealth.

—A. Carnegie

This chapter will discuss why the pension fund is often a corporation's most undermanaged "business." The term *business* applies because most employer retirement systems have the attributes of a financial subsidiary. This chapter also proposes a systematic approach to pension fund management. Finally, it offers an organizational model for the content of the rest of this book.

EMPLOYER PENSION PLANS: UNDERMANAGED SUBSIDIARIES?

Most enterprises—large and even not so large, private and public—have at least two important elements in common. First, they operate peculiar financial subsidiaries with very long-term liabilities. Second, these "businesses" are seldom managed with the same intensity and dedication devoted to the enterprises' main-line businesses.

The result is that some of these financial subsidiaries are undercapitalized; others are overcapitalized. Some have risk policies for the business that are, more through accident than design, inappropriate. Others have investment programs more likely to lose than add value to the "equity" in the business. Many have no established procedures to identify when things are going wrong in the business, what is going wrong, and what is needed to fix the problem.

None of this would matter much except for an important reality. These financial subsidiaries often exceed other subsidiaries or divisions of the enterprise in dollar value and in their potential impact on the enterprise's overall financial condition. Only a 1 percentage point increase in long-term return on assets of the subsidiary, for example, can produce an equivalent effect of reducing the subsidiary's debt obligations by 25 percent.

Such an event could well double the subsidiary's equity. As this equity is often significant in relation to regular balance sheet equity—indeed, it has been known to exceed it—the financial impact of this subsidiary on the main business is often considerable and sometimes dramatic.

These financial subsidiaries are the retirement plans of the enterprises. Most are based on pension benefit promises defined in absolute dollars or in relation to employees' earnings and length of service. These benefits, when earned, effectively become debt obligations of the enterprise. As pension debt accumulates it is funded; contributions and their investment return constitute the asset side of the retirement system balance sheet. These assets are available to retire pension obligations when they fall due.

Strangely, there is no standard way of determining by what amount pension assets should exceed pension liabilities—in other words, how the equity requirements of the financial subsidiary should be determined.

Not only is determining the appropriate equity levels in these businesses problematical, but balance sheet risk policy and investment organizational structure also cause pension plan sponsors considerable difficulty. Does the popular asset mix policy of 60 percent stocks–40 percent bonds really make good business sense, or is it simply a manifestation of communal safety-in-numbers behavior? Despite a specialization explosion in investment management services, the right formula for successful value-added investment management programs is as elusive as ever.

Finally, there is the problem of figuring out if the financial results from operations are good, bad, or indifferent. There is no lack of numbers; in fact, there are probably too many. Money managers, actuaries, accountants, custodians, and performance measurers can, and often do, produce numbers by the pound—quarterly, monthly, or any frequency you like.

But which ones are signals for change, and which ones are simply noise? Often the need to appear action-oriented produces decisions based on the latter, rather than the former. Investment program changes are invariably expensive; if they do not fix a problem, they are considerably worse than making no changes at all.

There is a common thread to these difficulties. Pensions have traditionally been a field dominated by outside agents. Pension plan sponsors—awed by the technical expertise of their asset-side and liability-side advisors—have often been decision takers when they should have been decision makers in matters of policy. Consequently, the critical asset cushion policy and asset mix policy decisions have frequently been made by outsiders.

Ironically, some sponsors have dabbled, on a part-time basis, in such operational areas as market timing and security selection. Decisions in these areas are best left to specialists equipped to deal with them on a dedicated, full-time basis.

Pension plan sponsors need a clearer perspective of where retirement systems fit into an overall corporate design. A guiding model or "paradigm" must be constructed to guide them in identifying the decisions they must make and those they should delegate. Such a model should lend itself to setting up guideposts for helping corporate managers make the decisions they must make themselves. It should also help them evaluate the decisions others should make on their behalf.

A PENSION PLAN PARADIGM: A CORPORATE FINANCIAL SUBSIDIARY

The goal of this book is both to provide a guiding model and to erect guideposts for those responsible for the financial management of employer pension plans. In suggesting pension plans are financial entities, we are providing a clue on where to start. The key to understanding a financial entity is understanding its balance sheet. Figure 1–1 shows how the pension plan balance sheet helps define what decisions must be made in organizing and operating a pension "business" and how these decisions relate to each other.

Figure 1–1 classifies the 15 dimensions of pension-system management as being asset-oriented, liability-oriented, or jointly asset/liability-oriented. It also classifies them as being planning-oriented, operations-

FIGURE 1-1 The Pension Plan Balance Sheet: A Guide to Organizing and Operating the Business*

	Asset-Oriented Policies and Functions	Asset/Liability-Oriented Policies and Functions	Liability-Oriented Policies and Functions
Planning	3 Asset mix policy 4 Investment management structure	2 Funding policy or asset cushion policy	1 Benefits policy
Operations	5 Staffing 6 Investment management 7 Asset custody and accounting	8 Employer and employee contributions	9 Employee communications 10 Benefit payments and administration
Control	11 Investment results monitoring 12 Asset mix policy, management structure staffing review and revision	13 Auditing, trusteeship, and compliance	15 Benefits policy review and revision

*All 15 dimensions noted on the balance sheet are further defined in the Technical Appendix to this chapter.

oriented, or control-oriented. The balance sheet device has already begun to help sort things out!

This book also uses Figure 1–1 as its organizational model. In subsequent chapters, *planning* will be the first order of business. Benefits policy and its implications for funding and investment goals is discussed, followed in turn by the two key financial policy issues: the size of plan assets in relation to plan liabilities (asset cushion policy), and the structure of plan assets (asset mix policy). The final planning chapter deals with the structure implications for establishing an effective investment management program.

The *operations* chapters deal with staffing the organization, running an investment management operation, and keeping track of the numbers and all the paper. These chapters recognize that only in very large pension funds is the "do it all yourself" option even feasible. Consequently, most of the discussion takes place in an external-manager/external-custodian context. However, while the operations practices might vary somewhat between internal and external implementation, the effectiveness principles are the same.

The *control* chapter focuses on understanding what information is worth looking at in trying to understand how the business is doing and how it can be organized most effectively. It also offers guidance on how results should and should not be used in order to review business policies, organizational structure, and staffing. A final chapter speculates on what may lie ahead for defined benefit employer retirement plans and their financial management.

Each chapter opens with a statement of issues and guiding principles pertinent to the chapter's subject matter. The application of the principles to the issues will be demonstrated through a case study approach. To ensure consistency and continuity, we decided to take a single plan sponsor—ALPHA Corporation—through the complete process of setting up and operating its pension plan "financial subsidiary." While ALPHA is not a real company, it could well be one. The corporation's characteristics, its problems, and their solutions have been drawn from actual cases familiar to the author.

As you, the reader, observe ALPHA's management systematically come to grips with the financial side of its retirement system, we hope that you will benefit from the experience. In the multimillion- and even multibillion-dollar businesses that retirement systems represent, even one new insight can make a measurable contribution to the bottom line of the "parent" company.

TECHNICAL APPENDIX
Fifteen Dimensions of Managing a Pension Subsidiary

1. **Benefits policy.** A dimension of overall corporate compensation policy that splits compensation into "now" and "later" parts. The "later" part becomes the debt of the pension subsidiary. From a financial viewpoint, it becomes critically important if pension benefits are defined in flat-dollar terms or as a percentage of final earnings and if any postretirement adjustments are promised. These factors determine to what degree pension debt is fixed-dollar debt and to what degree it floats with inflation.

2. **Asset cushion policy** (or funding policy). How much capital the business should have. The key issue is how large the asset cushion—the "equity" in the business—should be in relation to accrued pension debt.

3. **Asset mix policy.** The basic risk policy for the business. A risk-minimizing policy would maximize certainty about the future value of the "equity"—the asset cushion—in the business. A return-maximizing policy would attempt to maximize the future value of the equity. Safety or predictability would be of secondary concern. These two options are, of course, only the extremes in a continuum of risk/reward choices.

4. **Investment management structure.** The beliefs of the plan sponsor about the degree of pricing efficiency in various capital-market components, and the embodiment of these beliefs in an organizational structure. The active-passive and core-specialist splits are the critical elements of the structure.

5. **Staffing.** The process of hiring internal and external investment managers. Getting the goals and mandates right is critical here.

6. **Investment management.** The activity required to implement the asset mix policy and to meet the performance standards of the investment program.

7. **Asset custody and accounting.** The numerical and physical counterpart of the investment program and much more.

8. **Employer and employee contributions.** The dollar flow into the pension fund resulting from the accrual of pension benefits and from asset cushion policy and its year-by-year implementation.

9. **Employee communications.** For employees to value a retirement scheme as part of their overall compensation, they must understand it.

10. **Benefit payments and administration.** From a financial perspective, pension debt service.

11. **Investment result monitoring.** The calculation and presentation of investment performance and its attribution. Critical to this attribution is sorting out the impact of investment manager decisions, of plan sponsor policy decisions, and of capital market behavior in general.

12. **Asset mix policy, structure, and staffing review and revision.** The process of deciding what, if anything, needs fixing on the asset side of the business and doing it if required.

13. **Auditing, trusteeship, and compliance.** The responsibilities and routines related to ensuring the system operates in a legal and ethical manner.

14. **Actuarial valuations.** Calculations designed to estimate the "best estimate" financial status (balance sheet) of the pension plan, to establish a funding target consistent with corporate asset cushion policy, and to satisfy filing requirements with the regulatory authorities. These different purposes would likely lead to the assignment of different values to pension assets and liabilities.

15. **Benefits policy review and revision.** The process of deciding if the liability side of the business needs attention and taking action if required. Practically, a major review would probably take place only in conjunction with an overall compensation policy review. More routine reviews would likely center on the timing and size of inflation updates to pensions-in-pay.

PART TWO

Business Policy

CHAPTER TWO

Corporate Pension Funds: Getting the Goals Right

Speak thy purpose out, I love not mystery or doubt.

—Scott

In setting pension fund goals corporate managers must recognize their moral and legal obligation to make sure that the promise to pay pension benefits can be met. Providing this security must be the fund's primary goal. But corporate managers have a choice as to what means they employ in achieving the primary goal.

Managers must decide on the size of the pension fund in relation to the size of pension liabilities. They must also decide on the way the fund is to be invested. Choices exist for both the structure of pension fund assets and the intensity with which these assets are to be managed.

This chapter explores the question of goals and the means available to achieve them.

ASKING THE RIGHT QUESTIONS

The primary goal of a corporate pension fund is to secure the employer's promise to pay pension benefits. If this primary goal were the only goal, running the fund as a business would be very simple. A combination of assets well in excess of obligations and a low-risk investment policy would do the job nicely.

But, of course, creating financial security for the beneficiaries is not necessarily a pension fund's only goal. Managers of the sponsoring business have a mandate from their shareholders to maximize the value of the firm's equity. They would not be serving the owners of the firm to the best of their ability if they did not investigate ways in which the pension fund could contribute to this overall corporate goal while at the same time ensuring that the fund is securing the firm's pension payment obligations.

This dual-goal reality has given corporate managers a lot of difficulty. If the two goals are at odds—and at first blush, it appears as though they could be—corporate managers are in a conflict between acting as responsible fiduciaries on the one hand and as effective value creators for their shareholders on the other. Fortunately, the apparent dilemma is more imagined than real. A concrete goal resolution process can demonstrate this to be so.

Goal resolution involves answering three essential questions:

- What minimum dollars are required to achieve the primary benefit security goal?
- As a matter of policy, how much more than this minimum should we target to have in the pension fund?
- How aggressive should we be in attempting to earn a rate of return in excess of what the minimum risk policy would deliver?

While the questions are not easy, answering them well has a tremendous payoff. The answers go a long way toward setting pension fund goals that take into account the interests of both plan beneficiaries and owners of the enterprise.

Determining the Minimum Dollar Requirement

Determining the minimum dollar requirement can be divided into a two-step process. Building a model that projects the size and timing of benefit payments for plan members at any point in time is a task requiring a high level of mathematical and statistical expertise.

The projections not only depend on the plan text benefit provisions and formulas and accurate work force demographics data, but also on such experience assumptions as price and salary escalation, employee turnover, average retirement age, and mortality. Creating a mathematical model of a retirement system must take all these factors into account.[1]

The second step is to estimate the present value of these payment projections. Present value calculation is driven by two key experience

FIGURE 2-1 Calculating the Minimum Dollar Requirement

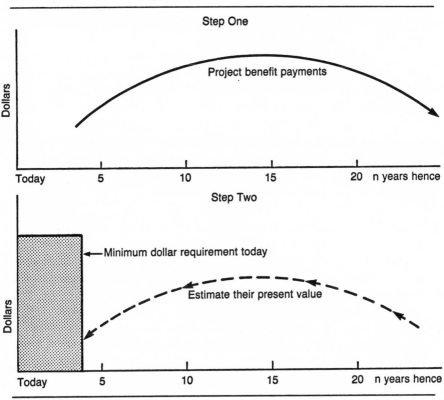

assumptions—both economic in nature. One is price and wage inflation experience. The other is what investments free of default risk might earn over the life of the payment obligations.

It is critically important that these economic projections be "best estimate" projections. That is, they should represent the most likely values that will actually be experienced—unbiased by our natural tendency to be conservative. We will see later that the funding process allows ample scope to build an asset cushion into the pension fund as a margin for error. However, unless the estimation process starts with best estimates, we'll never know what size errors to build margins for! Figure 2–1 shows the two-step process graphically.

The division of the liability valuation process into the two steps was done deliberately. Only step 1 requires special actuarial training, dealing as it does with such technical matters as expected employee group quit rates, retirement date behavior, and mortality rates. However, the second step of the valuation process has essentially a financial orientation, dealing as it does with future investment and inflation experience. In the age of the microcomputer, these second steps can be carried out on-site by corporate finance specialists rather off-site by actuarial consultants.

Note that the two steps imply a going-concern and not a wind-up valuation. Wind-up valuations estimate the minimum dollar requirement on the assumption that the plan is to be terminated. Hence, this type of valuation does not require the projection of retirement benefits based on final—and therefore higher—earnings than today. The minimum dollars required to fulfill the employer's funding obligation should reflect an ongoing plan in an ongoing corporation.

All this might seem elementary, almost self-evident. Yet many plan sponsors do not perform these best estimate valuations. Instead, they focus on the traditional "actuarial valuation" used for filing with the regulatory authorities. This "valuation"—a misnomer, really, if one goes by the dictionary meaning of the word—deliberately uses conservative assumptions for future returns and often uses conservative funding methods as well. Such conservative funding methods create an extra asset margin in the plan to ensure a smooth contribution rate even if the work force's average age rises.

This type of valuation produces a dollar value requirement—or "funding target"—that is not the minimum requirement. Rather, it is the minimum requirement plus a safety cushion of indeterminate size. Corporate managers who accept the dollar value based on the traditional actuarial valuation as the required fund value, without knowing what size cushion it implies, are delegating an important corporate finance decision to an outside consultant.

A recent study[2] on the financial status of private sector employer pension plans indicates almost 9 out of 10 funding targets for final earnings plans lie 30 to 60 percent above the minimum dollars required to meet ongoing—not wind-up—plan obligations. The median target was 38 percent greater than the minimum dollar requirement.

Figure 2-2 shows the relationships between the minimum dollar requirement, the funding target, and plan assets at market. The median results in the cited study are used; hence the relationships shown in Figure 2-2 should be representative for middle-of-the-road final earnings plans. They have been normalized in relation to $100 of the minimum dollar requirement.

What Figure 2-2 indicates is that the typical final earnings plan is targeting to have almost 40 percent more in assets than the going-

FIGURE 2-2   The Asset Cushion Concept

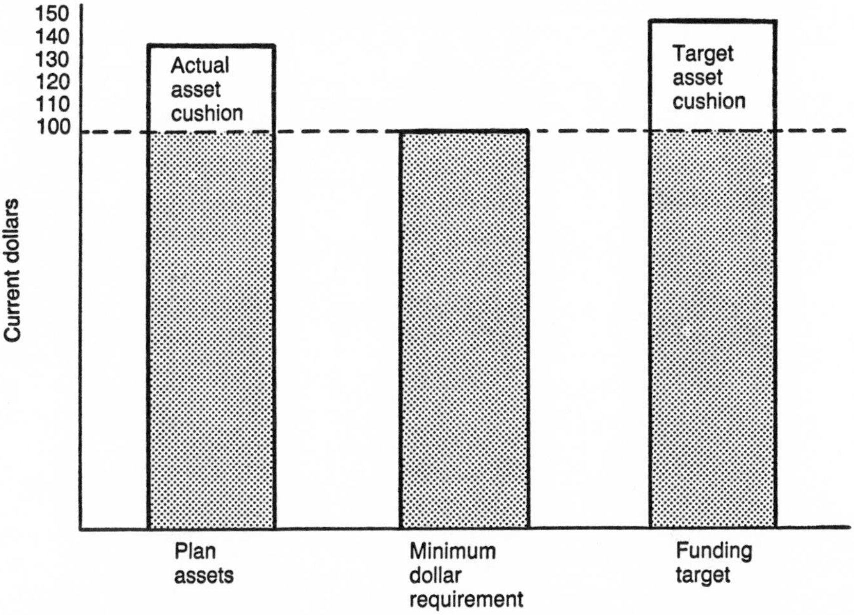

concern, best estimate, minimum dollar requirement. It also indicates that, at least at the time of the study, actual plan assets were marginally below the target level.

Study design was such that participants only supplied the plan asset values and funding target (or actuarial liability) values. Discussion with the study participants indicated few had any idea what the asociated minimum dollar requirement was. The implication is few had ever analyzed the question of appropriate asset cushion size.

How Much More Than the Minimum Dollar Requirement?

Surprisingly, few corporate managers have formally decided what their normal plan asset cushion should be. In other words, what size pension fund—relative to accrued pension obligations—is most appropriate in their plan and corporate context? Yet this decision, when carefully studied, touches a corporation's very identity and culture. The normal cushion issue goes well beyond such actuarial considerations as adverse employee turnover, retirement date, and mortality experience, as the following questions demonstrate.

- Are there any understandings about deferred compensation which are not explicitly written in the plan text? If so, is this implicit promise or contract to be funded?
- Is the fund to be managed to produce a rate of return in excess of what the minimum risk policy would produce? If so, should a reserve against adverse investment experience be established?
- Who owns the asset cushion? Are the legal and moral answers to this question the same? If the shareholders do own all or most of the cushion, how quickly could it be redeployed to meet other corporate financial needs?
- In fulfilling its duty to minimize the corporate tax bill, to what degree should management take into account the tax shelter and tax arbitrage opportunities the pension fund offers?
- The corporation probably has creditors other then its employees. To what degree should or must they be considered in setting the pension fund asset cushion policy?
- Finally, government-sponsored pension benefit insurance schemes offer employers the opportunity to "put" their accrued pension debt to the sponsors of solvent plans in return for the transfer of plan assets and part of the equity in the corporation. Should this option play any role in determining asset cushion size?

With a bit of organization, these questions can be fitted into a brief questionnaire that will quickly get senior management facing the key asset cushion policy issues (see Table 2–1).

While the questionnaire cannot determine an actual value for the target asset cushion (more on that in Chapter Three), the way in which the questions are answered should provide a clear indication as to whether a small or a large cushion is most appropriate for the corporation.

The smallest possible cushion would buffer the plan against adverse economic and noneconomic experience—return, inflation, turnover, retirement age, mortality—with only the minimum margin for error. The largest possible cushion would provide a buffer allowing for all conceivable errors and contingencies with its ceiling limited only by the government's willingness to extend tax-exempt status to the pension plan.

Figure 2–3 graphically displays the choices facing the corporation. Both the minimum and maximum funding targets are shown in relation to the minimum dollar requirement.

TABLE 2-1   Asset Cushion Policy Decision Questionnaire

Benefits Policy	Have we made implicit promises in addition to those stated in the plan text? Y/N If Y, should they be funded? Y/N
Cushion Ownership	Can we make decisions assuming the corporation owns all or most of the asset cushion? Y/N If Y, should we assume slow or fast recapture capability? S/F
Investment Policy	Do we have a pension fund return target in excess of what the minimum risk policy would produce? Y/N If Y, should we have a cushion component that would act as a buffer against adverse investment results? Y/N
Tax Policy	For the purpose of tax planning, should we integrate the pension plan and the rest of the corporation? Y/N
Other Creditor Relationships	Does the corporation's financial status in general affect asset cushion policy? Y/N If Y, does it make the recapture of the existing cushion unattractive? Y/N If Y, does it make the buildup of cushion impractical? Y/N
Pension Benefit Insurance	Does its existence affect the corporation's asset cushion policy? Y/N If Y, does it argue for a smaller or larger cushion? S/L

Before we turn our attention to ALPHA Corporation and see how its management deals with the asset cushion policy questions posed in Figure 2-3, let's first identify the same key questions related to investment policy.

Investment Policy: How Aggressive?

This question is best answered by first understanding the characteristics of the risk-minimizing investment policy for defined benefit employer pension plans. There are a number of considerations. First is the length and inflation sensitivity of the accrued pension liabilities. Next is the amount of credit and equity risk to be undertaken in investing the plan's assets. There is also the question of the investment style to be employed in managing the pension assets. We deal with each consideration in turn.

Nonfinancial businesses arrive at their desired capital structure by first deciding what assets they need to operate in their chosen field of business. Then they decide how to finance these assets through some

FIGURE 2-3 The Range of Asset Cushion Policy Choices

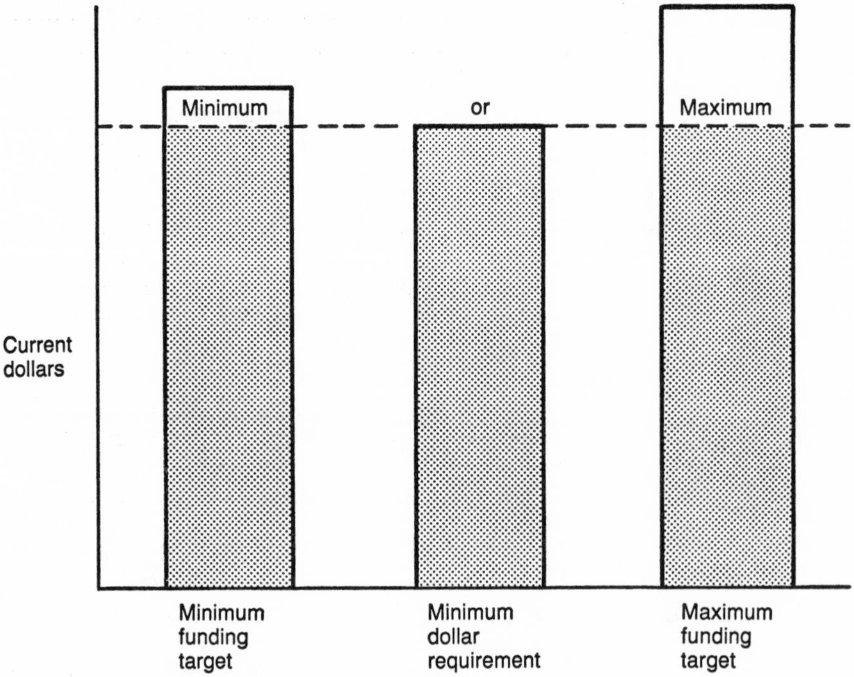

mix of debt and equity. Financial businesses usually reverse this procedure. That is, the debt is issued first—typically on top of a small equity base—and then the proceeds are invested, the goal being to earn a profit on the spread between the lending and borrowing rate.

A pension plan is a lot like a financial business. The employer issues payment promises to its employees, sets aside funds to secure the promise, and invests the funds until they are needed to meet the obligation.

Managers of financial businesses are acutely aware that their reserves—their asset cushion—can be eroded in two ways. First, a mismatching of the length and inflation-sensitivity of assets and liability payment terms creates risk exposure. Ask bankers how well they sleep at night when they lend long and borrow short! Second, investments can be subjected to default or equity risk. The same bankers will tell you that even sovereign credits don't always make their principal and interest payments when due!

So it is with pension plans. Their assets and liabilities can be matched or mismatched in length and inflation sensitivity. The purchase of anything other than default-free debt securities implies taking on default and/or equity risk. Finally, there is a third type of risk that financial businesses with marketable securities portfolios can take on.

Active management risk is incurred when asset managers attempt to outfox other asset managers. This activity, although presumably only undertaken with the expectation of adding to asset returns, obviously adds risk to the business. Not even the smartest foxes are right all the time.

These considerations help define what the risk-minimizing investment policy for defined benefit pension plans must look like. First of all, there is no active management—that is, no attempts are made to make money by trying to "buy low and sell high." Second, only the highest grade securities are held. Third, as much as possible, the length and inflation-sensitivity of the liabilities are matched by assets of equal length and inflation-sensitivity.

In the case of most defined benefit plans, some of the liabilities are fixed in dollar terms—usually moneys owing to plan members no longer active employees. The remaining liabilities—future pensions that have already accrued to still-active employees—are often tied to employees' final years' earnings, making them inflation-sensitive.

Finally, the reserves—the asset cushion—must also be invested. In the spirit of risk minimization, it should be highly liquid and not exposed to default risk. The result of following such a policy to the extreme is shown graphically in Figure 2-4. Again, typical proportions are shown, standardized on $100 of minimum dollar requirement.

Managers of financial businesses also know that a risk-minimizing investment policy is a low profitability policy. So it is with pension funds. Money—in an incremental return sense—can only be made by moving away from a passive, no-default risk, liability-matching investment policy.

In considering if, and to what degree, the pension fund should be assigned a mission to make money—that is, move away from the risk-minimizing investment policy—the question of asset cushion ownership must be addressed first. If shareholders do not receive the lion's share of rewards accruing from placing the pension fund at risk (assuming it backs defined benefit liabilities), there is no corporate rationale for doing so.

Ownership in this context does not necessarily imply being able to rapidly move the asset cushion out of the fund. Enjoying a lower, long-term contribution rate in the fund translates directly into a higher, long-term return on equity for corporate shareholders.

The next consideration affecting the degree to which investment policy might move away from the risk-minimizing position is the actual

FIGURE 2-4 The Risk-Minimizing Investment Policy

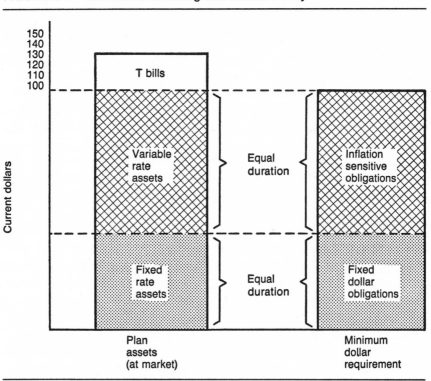

size of the asset cushion today. Closely related is the degree of flexibility permitted by regulators to smoothe the effects of year-to-year fluctuations in return and inflation experience.

This consideration assumes corporate managers attach value to short- and medium-term contribution predictability (experience shows that this predictability is indeed valued). Where this consideration is relevant, the larger the asset cushion, the more scope there will be for assuming pension fund investment risk today without having to worry about fluctuating pension contributions tomorrow.

Having established that investment risk can be undertaken and that its rewards would accrue to the shareholders, attention can turn to the types of risks that are worth undertaking. The concept of a market portfolio is useful here. It represents the portfolio held by the composite of all investors. In its broadest sense, it represents not only national stocks and bonds by their aggregate market value weights, but mortgages, real estate, venture capital, and international investments as well.

Such a portfolio's long-term real return should closely mirror the real growth in the world economy, possibly in the 2–3 percent per annum area. Because of the long-term nature of the liabilities involved and the existence of a substantial current asset cushion, the typical pension fund can probably absorb more investment risk than the composite investor, warranting a real return target in excess of 2–3 percent.

Two types of actions can lead to the achievement of a more ambitious target return than that implied by the market portfolio. One is to have a more aggressive asset mix policy—a policy involving the assumption of more default and equity risk than is being undertaken by the composite investor.

Such additional aggressiveness might warrant adding 1 to 2 percent to the, say, 2½ percent target associated with the market portfolio. This "reward" expectation is realistic if investors in general are risk-averse. Such attitudes along with reasonably efficient capital markets—a defensible assumption—systematically generate rewards for bearing risk.[3]

The other target return-raising action is the successful employment of active investment management services. Active management can focus on asset mix shifting or on specialized management within investment classes, such as own-country stocks, bonds, and bills, as well as those in international markets. Wherever employed, success means the generation of excess return—that is, return in addition to what a passively implemented policy would have produced.

The record shows that this source of excess return has been an elusive one for the majority of pension funds.[4] Given the incremental risks

---

TABLE 2-2 Investment Policy Decision Questionnaire

Asset Cushion Ownership	Can we make decisions assuming the corporation owns all or most of the asset cushion? Y/N
Minimum Risk Policy	Do we know the zero-default risk asset mix that best matches the length and inflation sensitivity of our pension obligations at this time? Y/N
Current Asset Cushion	Do we have a recent estimate of our actual asset cushion? Y/N
Asset Mix Policy	Are we prepared to take on default and equity risk in the fund in order to increase its return prospects? Y/N If Y, some of this type of risk or a lot? S/L
Investment Management	Do we believe active management can add value? Y/N Do we believe we can identify active managers who will be successful—before, rather than after, the fact? Y/N

FIGURE 2-5 Investment Policy Choices

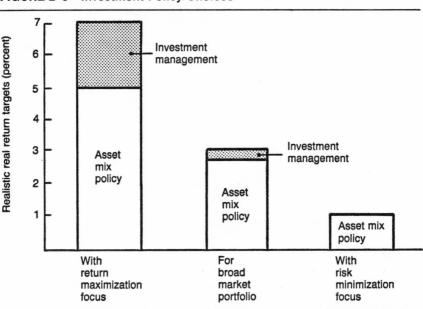

and administrative complexities involved, a target ½ percent (net of fees and transaction costs) contribution to total fund return should be capable of being justified if the pension fund is going to engage active investment management services.

While considerations impinging on investment policy decisions are fewer than those suggested for the determination of the asset cushion policy, taking the time to formally list the key questions is still useful. They appear in Table 2-2.

Just as the asset cushion decision table could not provide details on how to implement asset cushion policy, this table cannot provide the details on how to implement a chosen investment policy—more on that in Chapters Four and Five. However, the investment policy decision table answers should clearly establish the direction in which the fund's investment policy is heading.

Figure 2-5 summarizes the range of investment policy choices available—from one that focuses on risk minimization at one end to one that focuses on return maximization at the other.[5]

Note that the two extreme policies are return-maximizing and risk-minimizing in both the asset mix policy and investment management contexts. The middle policy is so in both contexts. Later chapters will develop a rationale for the magnitudes of the Figure 2-5 targets.

TABLE 2-3 Summary Balance Sheets of the Main and Pension Businesses

Assets		Liabilities	
Main business:		Main business:	
Current assets	$1.2 billion	Current liabilities	$0.6 billion
Fixed assets	$1.2 billion	Long debt	$0.8 billion
		Shareholders equity	$1.0 billion
Pension business:		Pension business:	
Pension Fund	$1.3 billion	Minimum dollar requirement	$0.9 billion
		Asset cushion	$0.4 billion

THE CASE OF ALPHA CORPORATION

ALPHA Corporation is a manufacturer of a broad range of consumer and industrial products. It operates a number of plants across North America and employs 20,000 people. The company has recently returned to a reasonable level of profitability after losing money during the severe recession that plagued the world economy at the turn of the decade.

The company is widely held with, interestingly, trusteed pension funds holding over half of the common shares. ALPHA's corporate culture emphasizes offering customers value for dollars, dealing fairly with its employees, and operating its businesses not only within the letter, but also within the spirit of the law.

As part of a renewed commitment by senior management to return the company to the high levels of profitability and common-share valuation enjoyed during the 1970s, it has decided to review all aspects of the company's pension plan. Recognizing that a review of overall benefits policy could not be conducted without addressing the even broader question of total compensation policy, management decided to tackle the narrower question of pension-related financial issues first. It started by summarizing the balance sheets of both the main business and the pension "subsidiary." This summary is shown in Table 2-3.

With a current share price of $30 and with 32 million shares outstanding, investors value the firm at $960 million.

ALPHA's Asset Cushion Policy

A quick examination of the balance sheet summaries reaffirms management's wisdom in tackling pension-related financial issues first. Pension

TABLE 2-4   Asset Cushion Policy Decision Table: ALPHA Corporation's Responses

Benefits Policy	**Have we made implicit benefit promises in addition to those stated in the plan text? Y/N** "Yes, we have. We have long had a practice of adjusting pensions-in-pay upwards, based on actual inflation experience. Our target is a 60 percent of CPI adjustment." **If Y, should they be funded? Y/N** "Because these adjustments are an important part of our overall compensation policy, we should budget for them and fund their accrual regularly over time, unless unusual circumstances prevent it."
Cushion Ownership	**Can we make decisions assuming the corporation owns all or most of the asset cushion? Y/N** "Yes we can. Even though, under normal circumstances, a good part of the cushion represents a reserve for benefit improvements, according to the plan text, we are not legally required to make these improvements. Also, we have not fallen into the trap of calling part of the contributions going into the plan *employee contributions.* The use of such a term when the employee has no say in the matter creates unnecessary ambiguity in some defined benefit plans."[6] **If Y, should we assume slow or fast recapture capability? S/F** "While we are prepared to quickly recapture the asset cushion by all legal means at our disposal in case of a corporate emergency, we would expect it more likely that any actual recapture would take place gradually through a reduction in the company's pension contributions."
Investment Policy	**Do we have a pension fund return target in excess of what the minimum risk policy would produce? Y/N** "Yes we do." **If Y, should we have a cushion component which would act as a buffer against adverse investment results? Y/N** "If we continue to pursue an investment policy geared to achieve a higher return than what the minimum risk policy would produce, we should maintain an asset reserve in the plan against adverse investment experience."
Tax Policy	**For the purpose of tax planning, should we integrate the pension plan and the rest of the corporation? Y/N** "Yes we should, but not to the degree where we can be accused of abusing the tax-exempt status of the company's pension plan to avoid paying corporate taxes."

TABLE 2-4   (continued)

Other Creditor Relationships	**Does the corporation's financial status in general affect asset cushion policy? Y/N** "No, our credit rating is good. Our financial advisors tell us we could finance our entire capital expenditure program via the capital markets without affecting our rating." **If Y, does it make the recapture of the existing cushion unattractive? Y/N** "Not applicable." **If Y, does it make the build-up of cushion impractical? Y/N** "Not applicable."
Pension Benefit Insurance	**Does the existence of pension benefit insurance affect the corporation's asset cushion policy? Y/N** "No." **If Y, does it argue for a smaller or larger cushion? S/L** "Not applicable."

---

assets are larger than either current assets or fixed assets of the main business. On a best estimate basis, pension debt is larger than either the current liabilities or long-term debt of the main business.

The asset cushion in the pension plan—on a before-tax basis, granted—equals 40 percent of shareholders' equity declared on the main business balance sheet. Management wondered how the firm's market value of $960 million might be affected if financial analysts became aware of its sizable pension asset cushion.

In order to systematically review what asset cushion policy would best serve the corporation in years to come, management decided to use the asset cushion decision questionnaire. Table 2–4 is a reproduction of the questionnaire and ALPHA's responses.

Table responses indicate ALPHA Corporation's asset cushion policy is going to tend toward the maximum end of the scale rather than the minimum required. With management deeming "other creditor" and "insurance" considerations to be irrelevant to their situation and deeming cushion ownership to be unambiguous, all other considerations favor a maximum asset cushion policy.

ALPHA's Investment Policy

Next, management used the investment policy decision questionnaire to examine its alternative with respect to the pension fund's investment policy.

TABLE 2-5 Investment Policy Decision Questionnaire: ALPHA
Corporation's Responses

Asset Cushion Ownership	**Can we make decisions assuming the corporation owns all or most of the asset cushion? Y/N** "Yes."
Minimum Risk Policy	**Do we know the zero-default risk asset mix that best matches the length and inflation sensitivity of our pension obligations at this time? Y/N** "Yes, this portfolio would have 15 percent in long-term, default-free, fixed-rate bonds, 55 percent in long-term, default-free, variable-rate bonds, and the rest in T-bills."
Current Asset Cushion	**Do we have a recent estimate of our actual asset cushion? Y/N** "Yes it is $400 million or 30 percent of assets."
Asset Mix Policy	**Are we prepared to take on default and equity risk in the fund in order to increase its return prospects? Y/N** "Yes we believe both the corporation and the pension fund have the financial strength to undertake such risk without endangering the benefit payment promises made." **If Y, some of this type of risk or a lot? S/L** "As much as can be taken without reducing the asset cushion below the minimum required level as determined by the actuary."
Investment Management	**Do we believe active management can add value? Y/N** "Yes." **Do we believe we can identify active managers who will be successful—before, rather than after, the fact? Y/N** "We are by no means certain we can. However, we are willing to take some calculated risks here. The fund's exposure to active management will be carefully controlled and monitored."

The responses indicate ALPHA's investment policy will be to reach out for a higher return target than what the minimum risk policy would produce.

ALPHA's Statement of Pension Fund Goals

With the directions of both asset cushion and investment policy clearly established, ALPHA Corporation is ready to write an initial draft of its statement of pension fund goals.

It is only a draft at this point because a detailed justification of the actual values used for return targets for the minimum risk policy and its

---

TABLE 2-6 The ALPHA Corporation Pension Fund: Statement of Goals

Fund goals:
- The primary purpose of the fund is to secure the benefit promises made by the corporation under the terms of its pension plan to its former and current employees.
- Subject to achieving this primary goal, the fund will be managed so as to make a measurable contribution to corporate profitability.

Means of achievement:
- The minimum dollar value of the fund required to secure accrued pension promises as set out in the plan text will be estimated annually using best estimate projections of return and inflation experience. Within its financial capability, the corporation will ensure that the market value of the fund exceeds this minimum value at all times.
- The corporation will establish—and review at least annually—its target asset cushion and the pace of moving toward it. In doing so, it will consider the following factors:
  —An adequate reserve against adverse plan experience of a noneconomic nature.
  —Anticipated updates of plan benefits.
  —The fund's investment policy.
  —Corporate tax considerations.
  —All relevant laws and regulations.
- The fund's investment policy will be structured so that the anticipation of a 4 1/2 percent long-term real rate of return is reasonable. This anticipation is based on an assumption of 2 1/2 percent long-term national income growth in real terms. Asset mix policy is to add 1 1/2 percent through the assumption of more equity risk than carried by the composite national market portfolio. The investment management program is to add an additional 1/2 percent through successful active management in a number of fund components.

---

two add-ons—related to asset mix policy and investment management structure—has yet to be made.

In making the major policy decisions summarized in the statement above, ALPHA's management had access to information and analyses that have not yet been described. These will be shared with the reader in the following three chapters.

But ALPHA has already traveled a long way. It has joined a still small group of plan sponsors and academics[7] working hard to understand the connections between corporate finance and pension finance.

As its statement of goals shows, the struggle has already begun to pay dividends for ALPHA. It has set a course that will lead to specific, knowledgeable decisions on how much of scarce corporate capital should be allocated to the pension business and how this money should be deployed.

CHAPTER NOTES

1. This book is not about actuarial methods or about the regulatory environment in which employer pension plans must operate. However, it is written keeping the realities of these elements and their impact on pension system financial management in mind. *Fundamentals of Private Pensions* by Dan M. McGill, published for the Pension Research Council by Richard D. Irwin of Homewood, Illinois, 1984, provides a great deal of detail on both actuarial methods and the U.S. regulatory environment.

   Understanding Pension Fund Finance and Investment by D. Don Ezra, published by Pagurian Press Limited of Toronto, Canada, 1979, gives actuarial methods a somewhat lighter treatment than the McGill book and also summarizes the Canadian regulatory environment. *The Financial Reality of Pension Funding under ERISA* by Jack L. Treynor, Patrick J. Regan, and William W. Priest, published by Dow Jones-Irwin of Homewood, Illinois, 1976, provides further detail on the historical evolution of employer plans and the regulations surrounding them.

2. This study encompassed 12 percent by number of plans and 20 percent by number of plan members of private sector trusteed plans in Canada. Plan data was mainly gathered from 1981 plan actuarial valuations. Due to the similarities between Canadian and U.S. actuarial methods and practices, the results are probably highly representative of U.S. plan experience at that time as well.

   The original motivation for the study was to estimate minimum dollar requirements related to accrued pension obligations so that realistic estimates of actual asset cushions in these plans could be estimated. This information was then used to estimate how much these cushions would decrease if certain government pension reform proposals were actually implemented.

   The study results were first presented to clients of Pension Finance Associates and members of the Financial Research Foundation of Canada, cosponsors of the study. They were published in book form by Pagurian Press in 1983. This book was authored by D. Don Ezra and titled *The Struggle for Pension Wealth*.

   Ezra and Ambachtsheer presented the study for the first time in the United States in October 1983 to the Institute for Quantitative Research In Finance. The institute announced in February 1984 that the study had won the 1983 Roger F. Murray Prize competition for best paper. A condensed version of the study appeared in the March–April 1985 issue of the *Financial Analysts Journal* under the title "*Private Pension Plans: Rich or Poor?*" Ezra and Ambachtsheer were coauthors of the article.

3. The most often-quoted work on estimating historical risk-premia is that of Roger Ibbotson and Rex Sinquefield. First published in 1977 by the Financial Analysts Research Foundation under the title, *Stocks, Bonds, Bills, and Inflation: The Past and the Future*, it has since been updated a number of times. The Canadian Institute of Actuaries regularly updates a Canadian equivalent of the original Study. The Canadian database was recently extended by James Hatch and Robert White in *Canadian Stocks, Bonds, Bills and Inflation: 1950–1983*, Financial Analysts Research Foundation, Charlottesville, Virginia, 1985.

   We continue to argue that there is considerable danger in blindly extrapolating the Ibbotson-Sinquefield results into the future. The last 60 years are *not* necessarily the best indicator of what the next 1, 5, 10, 20, or 60 years might bring. Our argument was twofold.

   First, the 53-year period originally studied was no more "normal" than any other period that could have been chosen. It contained 10 years of depression, 7 years of war (adding the Korean conflict to the World War II), maybe 30 years of basically good times—although much of it with a rising inflation bias followed by an inflation blowout still in progress at the time the original study ended. Before simply accepting these historical frequencies as best estimate probabilities looking forward, one really ought to pause, sit back, and think about how reasonable making such a leap is.

The second problem with blind historical extrapolation is that at least some of the actual asset class return behavior during the four types of capital market environments identified above is not likely to repeat itself. A good example is the behavior of the Federal Reserve Board in the late 1940s and early 1950s. It arbitrarily pegged interest rates at very low nominal levels during this period of relatively high inflation. What are the chances the Fed would set the T-bill rate at 2 percent tomorrow?

A second example is the secular change that has taken place in the makeup of the investing public over the last 60 years. The increasingly institutionalized nature of the savings process—with the appearance of trusteed pension funds possibly its most dramatic manifestation—has also had its impact. Do institutional investors require the same premiums for bearing equity risk as individuals? Probably not.

A "with-blinders-on" mind-set in using the Ibbotson-Sinquefield results will lead to a third problem. A pension fund that has not used asset classes other than stocks, bonds, and bills during the last 15 years has missed out on significant opportunities for return enhancement. Real estate, direct investments in small businesses, and international investments are but three important areas not covered by the original Ibbotson-Sinquefield work.

The importance of considering these areas is well made in a Winter 1983 *Journal Of Portfolio Management* article titled "The World Market Wealth Portfolio" by Roger Ibbotson and Laurence Siegel. The application of an expanded list of asset classes to pension fund management is further explored by Gary Brinson, Jeffrey Diermeier, and Randolph Hood in *Multiple Markets Index White Paper*, a First National Bank Of Chicago publication published in 1983.

4. Over a dozen studies show that, on average, professional investment managers have trouble outperforming passive capital market benchmarks. Most of these same studies also show that there is little period-to-period correlation between relative performance rankings.

   However, this evidence does not prove "value-added" investment management is either impossible to execute or to identify. Personal observation strongly suggests some of the foxes are foxier than others. It also suggests environmental conditions are extremely important; no fox survives long when taken out of its natural element. These observations will be expanded into full-length chapters further on in the book.

5. The suggested targets for the three types of asset mix policies draw heavily on the observations made and the studies cited in note 3 above. They do not, however, come from a single historical source or theoretical derivation.

6. We admit to putting words in the mouths of ALPHA's management on the employee contribution question. There is, of course, only a trivial economic difference between a noncontributory defined benefit plan and a contributory defined benefit plan where the employee is given no choice but to contribute. In both cases, the employer is obliged to pay a defined benefit. In both cases, the employer pays the same total compensation. In both cases, the employee ends up receiving the same amount of money as current compensation.

However, the psychological difference can be enormous. In the contributary plan case, the illusion is created that money contributed into the plan by employees is employee money that should fully share in any investment success the fund has (the allocation of investment losses is never discussed). The resulting cost to employers can be considerable—in employee mistrust when it is discovered their contributions earn a "scandalous" 5 percent, or in time and energy spent trying in vain to explain why the 5 percent might be in fact fair.

7. Probably the best publication at this time setting out how far academia has come in understanding pension finance and investments is the National Bureau Of Economic Research's *Financial Aspects of the United States Pension System*. Edited by Zvi Bodie and John Shoven, it was published by the University of Chicago Press in 1983.

Many of the academia's best finance and investment thinkers—Myron Scholes, Bill Sharpe, Ben Friedman, Fisher Black, Martin Feldstein, Jim Pesando, Irwin Tepper, and Jay Light, among them—have their say in this book either as a paper contributor or as a discussant. In light of the brilliance of their analyses—much of which focuses on corporate sponsors of defined benefit pension systems—the following summary remarks are revealing.

By Irwin Tepper: "to date, the theory of optimal pension policy is . . . obviously at odds with practice."

By Jay Light: "for the present, however, we are left in a somewhat unsatisfactory state . . . our evolving theories on pension policy and our evolving understanding of reality are at odds with one another in several important respects."

The theories Tepper and Light are referring to treat the sponsor and the pension plan as one integrated whole. Following through both asset cushion policy and investment policy to their theoretical extremes, total integration does indeed suggest extreme policies. Cushions should be either maximized or minimized in size. Investment policies should be either return-maximizing or tax-minimizing or risk-minimizing.

In fact, as both Tepper and Light observe, very few plan sponsors behave that way. It would be a mistake to suggest that this either makes the sponsors wrong and the academics right—or vice versa. Rather, it suggests an important opportunity for sponsors to learn from academia—and vice versa.

Indeed, in writing *Pension Funds and the Bottom Line* we have attempted to use some of the good ideas that have come out of evolving pension policy theory. However, by having ALPHA's very practical management team decide which ideas to use—and how—we have hopefully integrated theory with the realities of running a large business enterprise.

CHAPTER THREE

Asset Cushion Policy: How Much Capital for the Pension Plan?

Keep no more cats than can catch mice.

—*Old English Proverb*

Deciding on the capital structure for the pension business is no easier or harder than it is for the plan sponsor's other businesses. What is different about the pension business decision is that it is often delegated to outside consultants.

This chapter shows how the plan sponsor can regain control of the capital structure decision. The chapter then takes the reader through a checklist to help decide if the pension plan asset cushion should be as small as possible, as large as possible, or somewhere in between these two extremes.

WHAT IS ASSET CUSHION POLICY?

Asset cushion policy reflects the pension plan sponsor's intentions regarding the relationship between assets and liabilities on the pension plan balance sheet. In Chapter Two we described the policy options as ranging from asset cushion maximizing to asset cushion minimizing. Stated differently, the fundamental issue is whether to cover the accrued pension debt with the largest pension fund possible, the smallest fund possible, or one somewhere in between.

This chapter explores these policy options and their implementation further. This exploration will lead to an occasional lapse into actuarial technicalities. However, the focus will continue to be the critical issue of allocating corporate financial resources to maximize corporate share value—subject to adequately securing accrued pension debt.

Readers are probably more familiar with the term *funding policy,* which is often used to denote the asset cushion policy concept. We prefer the latter term as it is less likely to be confused with a host of actuarial concepts and tools—funding methods, funding targets, actuarial cost methods, actuarial liabilities, and so on—which tend to be means to achieve certain ends rather than the ends themselves.

The Range of Asset Cushion Policy Options

We noted previously that the pension subsidiary is *liability driven*—that is, pension liabilities are created as part of an overall corporate compensation package first, and these liabilities are then funded. The present value of these liabilities—the accrued pension debt—can be estimated at any point in time.

By using best estimate rather than conservatively biased return and inflation assumptions along with equally unbiased work force specific assumptions, the best estimate of the accrued pension debt can be calculated. We have already called this estimate the *Minimum dollar requirement.* It is the bare bones liability but a going-concern liability in the sense that it includes inflation projections when the plan text promises final earnings related benefits.

Asset cushion policy then is the desired—or target—level of plan assets in relation to this estimate liability value, as shown in Figure 3-1. It is implemented by establishing a funding target—unfortunately often called the *actuarial liability*—through the choice of a set of actuarial methods and assumptions that produce the desired target value. The resulting enlarged liability—the funding target, really—is thus made up of two components: the minimum dollar requirement plus the target asset cushion.

If the actual asset cushion—easily established by comparing plan assets at market to the minimum dollar requirement—is less than the target cushion, extra pension contributions (that is, extra to the contributions related to normal cost) are triggered. Conversely, if the actual cushion exceeds the target cushion, a state of declared surplus is said to exist, giving rise to the opportunity to reduce contributions below the normal cost rate.

Setting the median minimum dollar requirement for final earnings plans in the previously cited study[1] at $100, its funding target was 38 percent higher at $138. With actual plan assets at $132, its actual asset

FIGURE 3-1 The Asset Cushion Concept

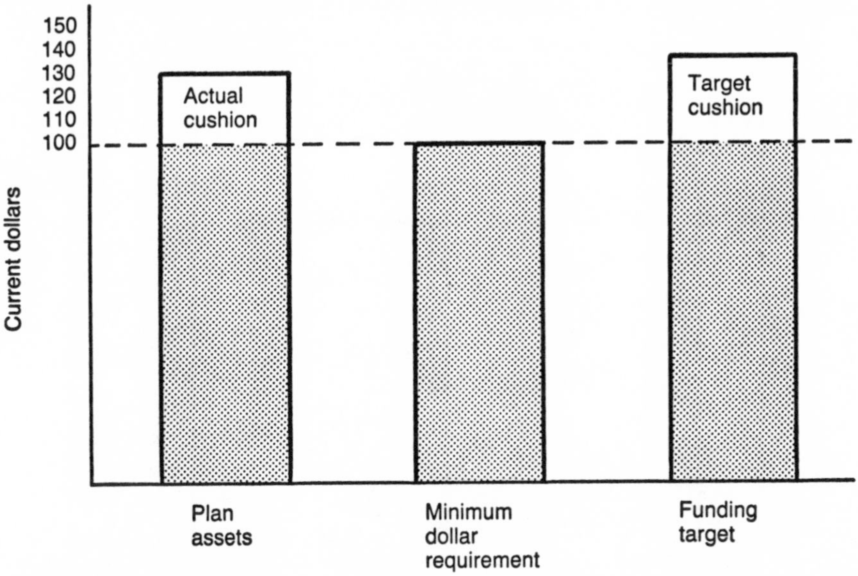

cushion was $6 below the apparently desired level. We explain later in the chapter why "desired" might describe reality less accurately than possibly "believed to be required" might.

To review then, there is by definition no asset cushion in the minimum dollar requirement estimate. If plan assets at market exceed the minimum dollar requirement, the plan has a positive actual asset cushion. The target asset cushion falls out of the difference between the funding target—sometimes called the *actuarial liability*—and the minimum dollar requirement. In Figure 3-1 the actual cushion was $32, the target cushion $38.

With the asset cushion concept established, the policy question is obvious: should we, the plan sponsor, target for the minimum or maximum cushion acceptable and/or allowable? Or somewhere in between? This question is posed graphically in Figure 3-2.

Taking into account both actuarial practices and regulatory constraints, answers to the minimum or maximum question will probably fall in the $120 and $180 range. In other words, it would be difficult—both as a practical and ethical matter—to establish a funding target that exceeded the minimum dollar requirement by less than 20 percent. At the other extreme, a funding target more than 80 percent above the

FIGURE 3-2 The Range of Asset Cushion Policy Choices

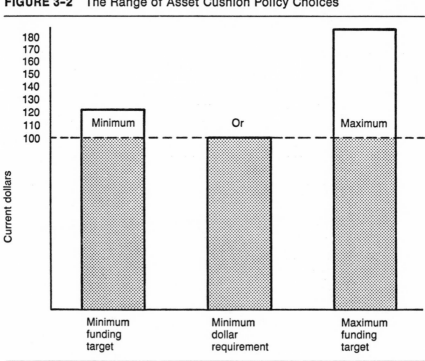

minimum dollar requirement becomes difficult to justify in margin-of-safety terms[2].

These benchmarks relate to final earnings plans. Significantly higher targets are justifiable for career average and flat benefit plans where active member benefits are not explicitly tied to final—or best year—earnings but where regular benefit updates are made. While these plans do not formally promise benefits related to final earnings, there is often an understood intent to do so by the employer. Such an intent should have a financial counterpart in funding policy.

Why Not the Minimum Asset Cushion?

Chapter Two listed six considerations in establishing an appropriate cushion policy. The considerations either push the sponsor in the direction of a cushion-minimizing policy or away from it. Table 3-1 summarizes the circumstances that would push or pull a plan sponsor towards the cushion-minimizing or maximizing ends of the spectrum.

Why not necessarily a policy that minimizes the asset cushion? Table 3-1 shows that benefits policy, investment policy, and tax policy

TABLE 3-1 Six Asset Cushion Policy Considerations

	Towards maximum if:	*Towards minimum if:*
Benefits Policy	There are implicit promises, probably related to inflation updates—post-retirement for final earnings plans and pre- and post for flat benefit and career average plans.	All benefits likely to be paid are stated in the plan text.
Cushion Ownership	The cushion belongs to the corporation.	The cushion belongs to the plan beneficiaries.
Investment Policy	Policy has return-maximizing focus.	Policy has risk-minimizing focus.
Tax Policy	Policy is to use every legal means available to minimize the overall corporate tax liability.	Policy is to treat the pension plan totally separate from the main business, including tax considerations.
Other Creditor Relationships	Relationships with nonpension creditors are unaffected by asset cushion decisions. Worthwhile capital expenditures can be financed without recourse to plan contributions or current asset cushion.	Nonpension creditors are insisting on a higher level of debt service and less leverage on the main business balance sheet. Worthwhile capital expenditures can be made but can not be financed.
Pension Benefit Insurance	The company does not expect to ever have to, or want to, turn the corporate plan over to a public guarantor.	It is quite possible the company might have to "put" the plan to a public guarantor some time in the future[3].

could directly argue against the advisability of such a policy. At the same time, the other three considerations—which could possibly argue in the opposite direction—are possibly only relevant to a minority of defined benefit pension plan sponsors.

Actual Corporate Pension Balance Sheets and Funding Targets

Figure 3-1 suggested actual funding targets lie, considerably above minimum dollar requirements. In the study this summary result came

FIGURE 3-3   Final Earnings Plan Financial Status Range

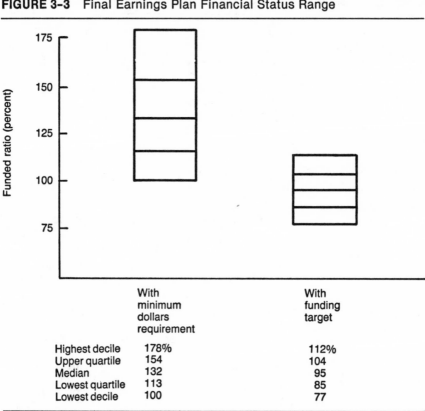

	With minimum dollars requirement	With funding target
Highest decile	178%	112%
Upper quartile	154	104
Median	132	95
Lowest quartile	113	85
Lowest decile	100	77

from[1] final earnings plans were found to have funding targets 30 percent to 60 percent above the estimated minimums required, with the median at 38 percent above. The comparable range for career average plans was 80 percent to 190 percent above. Interestingly, flat benefit plan funding targets were in a much narrower 90 percent to 100 percent above minimum required range.

Given the first consideration above—benefits policy—these higher ratios in career average and flat benefit plans, which do not automatically adjust the benefits of even active employees for inflation, are not surprising. The target asset cushion policies here generally anticipate inflation-related benefit updates to active employees. These anticipations are reflected in the much higher funding targets in relation to minimum dollar requirements which do not reflect future inflation. Such pre-retirement updates are, of course, automatic in final earnings plans.

The range of actual experience in the study for final earnings plans is shown in Figure 3-3. All data are expressed in terms of funded ratios in this graph—the ratio of plan asset values (always at market) to the minimum dollars required liability and the actuarial liability (or, more accurately, the funding target). The numbers can be thought of as representing the plan asset value per $100 of minimum dollars required and per $100 of funding target, respectively.

There are a number of results in Figure 3–3 worthy of special attention:

- The $132 asset position relative to the $100 minimum dollar requirement for the median plan previously represented in Figure 3–1 shows up as a 132 percent funded ratio in Figure 3–3.
- On a minimum dollar requirement basis, only the bottom 10 percent of the sample was not fully funded, that is, did not have plan assets in excess of this amount. The implication is that even final earnings defined benefit plans—the type of plan with the highest per employee pension liability—were generally well-funded—at least at the time of the study, the 1981–82 period.
- The funded ratio range that uses the funding target—or actuarial liability—as its denominator is relatively narrow, with the median plan being declared to have plan assets 95 percent of the size of the funding target. In other words, over 50 percent of the plans in the sample were not only making their normal contributions relating to current service, they were also making extra contributions in order to raise their asset cushions above current levels.

In order to see what level of postretirement inflation protection the target asset cushions might afford, the minimum dollar requirements were reestimated in the study—but now with the provision that first 50 percent, and then 100 percent of CPI protection had to be prefunded. Figure 3–4 shows how the results were affected.

From these additional results it is clear that:

- Only the top 10 percent of plans in the sample had sufficient assets to fully secure a 100 percent of CPI postretirement inflation update promise.
- The funded ratios that use the funding target as the denominator correspond most closely to the funded ratios that have the minimum dollar requirement + 50 percent of CPI denominator. One might infer from this that most final earnings plan funding targets point toward a benefits policy that strives to update pensions for half of the inflation rate—without formally promising to do so. However, while such funding and benefits policies might well be appropriate, we suspect that the observed results are due more to

FIGURE 3-4 Final Earnings Plan Financial Status Range with Prefunded Inflation Protection

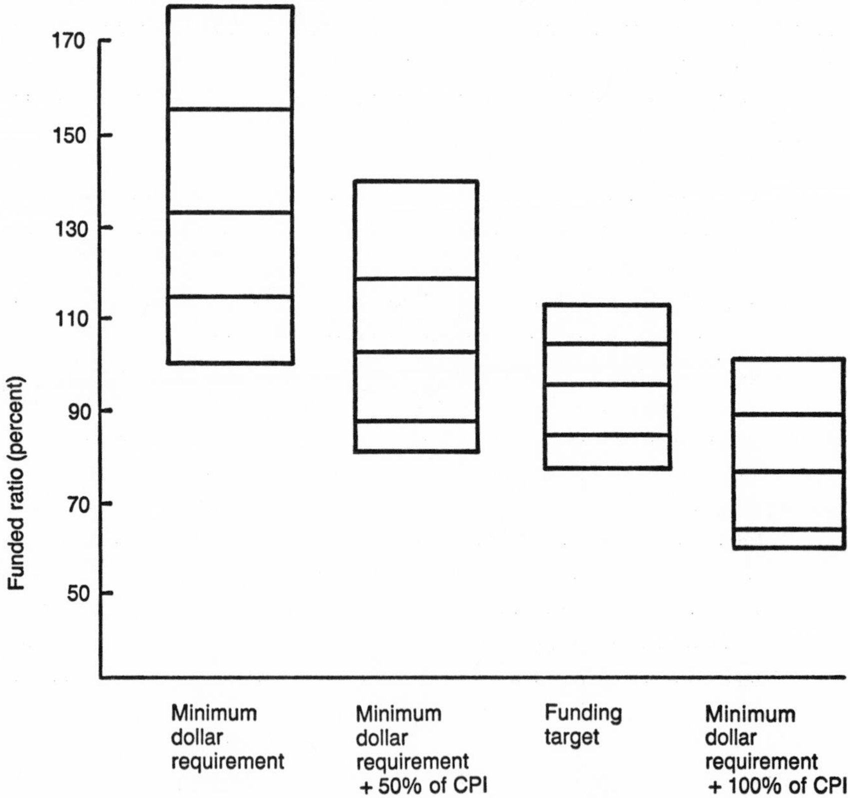

	Minimum dollar requirement	Minimum dollar requirement + 50% of CPI	Funding target	Minimum dollar requirement + 100% of CPI
Highest decile	178%	140%	112%	102%
Upper quartile	154	117	104	89
Median	132	102	95	76
Lower quartile	113	87	85	64
Lowest decile	100	81	77	60

adherence to historical convention and rules of thumb than they are to the outcomes of consciously thought-out policies.

Actual Asset Cushions: Results of Conscious Policy?

No doubt some pension plan sponsors do think their way through the maximum/minimum target cushion question. After deciding on the asset cushion most appropriate for them, they instruct the plan actuary to implement the resulting policy using assumptions and techniques deemed acceptable by both actuaries themselves and by the regulatory and tax authorities.

However, for every such plan sponsor there is at least one other—maybe even two or three others—where no formal asset cushion policy has ever been established. Instead, the term **actuarial liability** is taken quite literally, with any asset shortfall relative to this "liability" believed to be a genuine "deficiency."

How has this common misconception arisen? The main villain in the piece is inflation. Actuarial techniques originated in the insurance industry, where they were typically applied to fixed-dollar liabilities in a low inflation, low interest rate environment. At first the transition of these techniques to pension plans was simple and painless—while both inflation and interest rates remained low and stable.

Then along came the late 1960s and the 1970s with their increasing and unstable inflation and interest rates. Quite logically, actuaries believed that in these conditions pension plans should build up a margin of safety against increasingly uncertain investment returns and inflation experience.

The misconception is reinforced by a multitude of publications which, not having access to comparable minimum dollar requirement values, publish lengthy tables of noncomparable funding targets or actuarial liabilities. This is usually accompanied by commentary that implies actuarial liabilities and minimum dollar requirements are equivalents[4].

While it is impossible to criticize the actuarial profession for wishing to safeguard the benefit security of plan members during uncertain times, possibly the same cannot be said for the means they chose to do so. As the interest rate yield curve rose steadily through the 1960s into the 1970s and 1980s, their interest rate assumptions used to discount projected benefit payments did not move up in tandem.

Interest rate assumptions at half the going market rate might be defended as realistic for discounting benefit payments either beyond the reach of bond durations or subject to inflation adjustment. The same cannot be said when the benefit payments are fixed in current dollars and within the reach of being matched by available fixed-income instruments.

In the latter situation the resulting liability calculation—the funding target—overstates the best estimate liability. A goal of the study cited above[1] was to ascertain to what degree this process had led to the build-up of asset cushions in pension plans by the early 1980s—the time period in which the study was performed.

It is in this context that the practice of "immunization" is best understood. **Immunization**—the explicit matching of fixed-dollar plan assets and liabilities—provides the actuary with a formal rationale to use a best estimate rather than an artificially low return assumption for the immunized liabilities. With a part of the asset cushion so released, it can be recaptured or, more likely, used to alter the sponsor's contribution rate into the plan[5].

Such a plan sponsor reaction to the discovery that the plan has an asset cushion already in place could be as undesirable as the process that put the cushion there in the first place. Much better to stop and think through the appropriate asset cushion policy for the plan and for the sponsoring corporation first. ALPHA's management heartily agreed with this viewpoint.

THE FINANCIAL STATUS OF ALPHA CORPORATION'S PENSION PLAN

ALPHA's management was well aware of the steady trend among plan sponsors towards increased use of bond immunization techniques to release part of the asset cushion in the pension plan. Indeed, this trend played an important part in their decision to establish an explicit asset cushion policy.

Management's first step was to ask their consultants[6] to give them an up-to-date picture of the plan balance sheet. Against plan assets of $1.3 billion, they specifically wanted to know their minimum dollar requirement with no postretirement indexing and with 60 percent of CPI indexing. They instructed that these values be estimated using near-term and far-term horizons for the key return and inflation projections.

The near-term should recognize the ability to lock up a known rate of return—the going yield to maturity on long-term (eight-year duration) government bonds—in relation to the plan's fixed-dollar debt to pensioners and other inactive plan members. The far term should employ "normal" relationships between fund return and price and wage inflation—recognizing that even normality is ultimately only a subjective notion.

In addition to these two minimum dollar requirements, management wanted to have the consultant's estimate as to what defensible minimum and maximum target asset cushions might be. By *defensible* they meant that the resulting funding target would be acceptable to the regulatory and tax authorities and also not in violation of standards set by the actuarial profession.

Figure 3-5 summarizes part of the resulting consultant's report. The graph displays the two minimum dollar requirements and the current funding target.

FIGURE 3-5 ALPHA's Current Financial Status and Funding Target

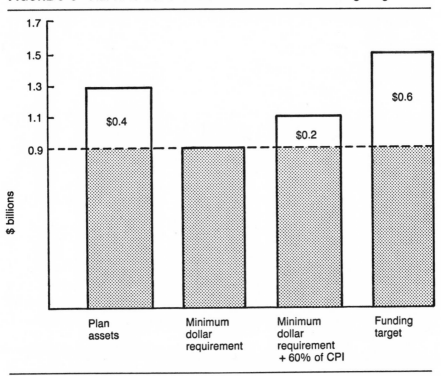

The results show ALPHA's pension financial subsidiary to be in excellent financial health, with the current practice of 60 percent of CPI updates to pensions-in-pay already funded. They also show that the current funding target has the plan on its way—barring poor investment results—to even better financial condition.

Management was, of course, aware that they had consented to make supplementary pension plan contributions at the time of the last actuarial valuation—2.5 percent of payroll in addition to the 7 percent related to current service. They recognized, however, that there was no explicit asset cushion policy in place at the time that the inplace funding track was established.

There was one further analytical result needed before any policy decisions could be made. What were the minimum and maximum feasible funding targets? By "feasible" management meant funding targets that could actually be set within existing rules, regulations, and practices. Figure 3-6 depicts the consultant's estimate of the range of feasible funding targets, contrasted with ALPHA's current funding target.

The minimum and maximum targets are approximately 20 percent and 80 percent, respectively, above the minimum dollar requirement—

FIGURE 3-6 Range of Feasible Funding Targets for ALPHA

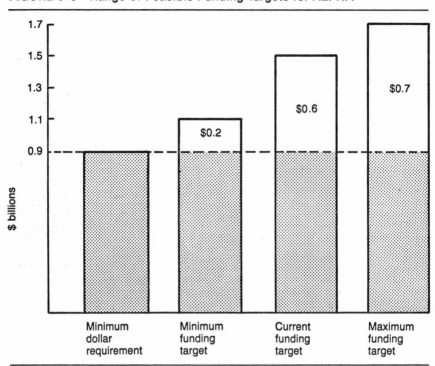

no CPI update. The minimum target could be implemented by immunizing the fixed-dollar liabilities with a dedicated bond portfolio and assuming 8½ percent/6½ percent (return/salary escalation) experience for the variable dollar liabilities.[7] Pension debt would be funded as it accrued—implying the use of a single premium or unit credit funding method.

By contrast, the maximum target could be implemented by projecting a 5 percent rate of return for all plan assets and 4 percent salary escalation for active employees. Alternatively, somewhat higher economic assumptions could be used, but a more conservative view could be taken of the value of plan assets, of employee turnover, of plan member mortality, etc. Pension debt would be funded on a level cost basis—implying the use of one of the funding methods that projects the total benefit to be paid at retirement and then allocates its cost evenly over the working life of the employee.[8]

The consultant pointed out that, while there were ways of further reducing the minimum target or increasing the maximum target, doing so would take ALPHA out of the broad (and broad it is!) band of actual current practices. It would also take the plan out of the range of practices consistent with the spirit in which defined benefit employer pension plans were established and are being regulated.

On the minimum side, questions start to arise about the employer acting in good faith with respect to its employees and plan benefit guarantors. On the maximum side, questions start to arise about possible abuse of the tax-exempt status of the plan through arguably sheltering not only plan income, but corporate income as well.

ALPHA's Deliberations on Asset Cushion Policy

In the process of establishing the fund's purposes and goals, the company already set the direction for its asset cushion policy. Management decided to review its responses to the asset cushion policy decision table.

These combined considerations clearly point ALPHA in the direction of having a large rather than a small asset cushion in its pension plan. But *how* large? For further guidance on this question management decided to place its current financial status and funding target in the context of the sample of final average plans in the previously cited financial status study.

Figure 3–7 suggests ALPHA's plan is currently already better funded that the typical final earnings plan in the sample on a comparable minimum dollars required basis. It falls in the second quartile—no CPI update basis—to first quartile break—50 percent CPI update basis. By contrast, it falls in the low third quartile on a funding target basis.

ALPHA's management was fascinated to discover the implications of this low third quartile ranking. While based on actual plan assets and minimum dollar requirement, their funded ratio ranked high, their high current funding target—officially called the **actuarial liability** in the plan valuation—made them appear to rank low! Further, they realized, that might very well be exactly where they want the plan to rank.

This thought led them to the next question in their quest for the most appropriate asset cushion policy. If we were already at our current $1.5 billion funding target, where would we rank then on the minimum dollar requirement scale? Now the answer surprised them.

A funded ratio of 167 percent on a no-CPI update basis and of 136 percent on a 50 percent update basis would move ALPHA's plan to almost the first decile break in the sample. In other words, the already in-place funding policy has the plan on a track to an asset cushion size that will—barring poor investment results or unanticipated benefit enhancements—eventually place it in the top 10 percent of a representative sample of final earnings plans.

TABLE 3-2 Review of Questionnaire Responses

Benefits Policy	Our compensation philosophy over the years has been to have our pension benefits rank in the top half of representative surveys. We have also adjusted our pensions in pay regularly for 60 percent of the CPI. This philosophy is still in place and should be reflected in our funding policy.
Cushion Ownership	There is nothing in the plan text to contradict our position that plan assets in excess of the minimum dollar requirement plus a contingency cushion—possibly 20 percent of the minimum dollar requirement—are effectively corporate assets deployed in its pension plan financial subsidiary. It is at management's discretion to decide if these assets are to remain in the plan—providing an extra margin of safety to plan beneficiaries and plan benefit guarantors—or potentially prefunding future benefit improvements. It is also at management's discretion to use the excess cushion (i.e., in excess of the 20 percent contingency cushion) to reduce the company contribution rate into the plan—or, in case of serious corporate financial distress, to even recapture part of the cushion for redeployment in our main business.
Investment Policy	We have decided to strive to earn a 4 1/2 percent long-term real rate of return through having both an asset mix policy that leans towards return maximization and an investment management program that involves a degree of active management. Both of these dimensions involve the assumption of a degree of incremental pension fund value volatility. The larger the asset cushion, the smaller the chance that a decline in fund value will lead to an unanticipated increase in the company contribution rate.
Tax Policy	We have no hesitation in being aggressive in minimizing our overall corporate tax liability. However, we do not want to abuse the tax-exempt nature of the pension plan by using it to achieve totally unrelated corporate goals.
Other Creditor Relationships	Interest coverage of our outstanding debt is excellent. Our underwriters tell us we could do a sizable new bond issue without any effect on our credit rating. This area is not a constraint on any asset cushion policy decision we make at this time.
Pension Benefit Insurance	As a strong, going-concern company with a long record as a good employer and a good corporate citizen, its existence is of little relevance to us. We do not expect our employees to ever be in a position where our plan can not meet its obligations. We do not intend to "game" the regulations by "going for broke" through running a negative asset cushion* high risk investment policy plan.

FIGURE 3-7   Final Earnings Plan Sample and ALPHA Corporation

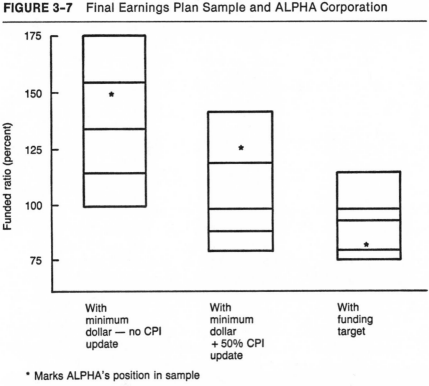

* Marks ALPHA's position in sample

While the six asset cushion policy questionnaire considerations support a large asset cushion policy, two further considerations were raised that made ALPHA wonder if it might not be overreaching with its current funding track. Both considerations related to the consequences of the eventual visibility of the asset cushion.

To what degree would the spreading knowledge of ALPHA's large and increasing pension fund asset cushion lead to demands for higher plan benefit levels? To what degree would the large cushion attract the attention of corporate raiders—bent on stripping assets, including pension plan asset cushions, from their acquisition targets?

Management decided they would establish ALPHA's asset cushion policy using the analytical framework in which the research on plan financial status and asset cushion target options had been carried out. Their thought process is presented in Table 3-3.

ALPHA Corporation's Asset Cushion Policy Decision

Table 3-3 is a continuation of the asset cushion policy questionnaire first introduced in Chapter Two. While Part 1 established a direction for

TABLE 3-3 Asset Cushion Policy Questionnaire: Part 2

Consideration:	Addition (percent)	Addition ($ billions)
Minimum dollar requirement	100%	$0.90
Minimum liability cushion	10	$0.09
60% CPI updates	25	$0.23
Aging work force reserve	10	$0.09
Reserve for investment policy risk	20	$0.18
Totals	165%	$1.49

the policy, Part 2 is geared to come up with an actual number. It starts with the minimum dollar requirement as the funding target base and then permits the addition of asset cushion components related to benefits policy, investment policy, and other cushion size considerations.

To management's surprise the questionnaire's $1.49 billion funding target worked out to be the actual funding target established at the last formal plan valuation—although without the benefit of the table or the decision framework it represents. However, they astutely recognized that by adding all the reserve components together they were effectively assuming all contingencies could occur simultaneously.

In fact, at least some of the contingencies against which reserves are being established would appear to be totally unrelated—bad investment results and a suddenly aging work force, for example. Consequently, if all the component margins were approximately right, their sum will be too large by some not easily determined amount.[2]

Referring back to the final earnings plan component of the financial status study[1], they recalled that the first quartile break funded ratio—using the minimum dollar requirement as the denominator—was about 150 percent. In light of all the analyses performed, that seemed like the appropriate target for ALPHA Corporation. It is 15 percentage points below the 165 percent that came out of the decision table—justifiable for reasons cited above—but still a full 50 percent above the minimum dollar requirement.

Only about 25 percent of final earnings plans appear to be in better financial condition than this standard signifies. Also, the 150 percent is only marginally above ALPHA's actual current funded ratio—using actual plan assets at market—of 144 percent. A reduction in required contribution rate—currently 2.5 percentage points above the 7 percent of payroll "normal" rate—of about two percentage points is implied.

Management realized that, given their current accounting practices, such a reduction in the contribution rate was equivalent to an increase in pretax earnings of $13 million or 40 cents per share. While they realized that this should not impact ALPHA's $30 share value, they suspected that the current share price did not totally reflect ALPHA's strong pension balance sheet. A reduction in the contribution rate could well signal this reality to financial analysts.[9]

In instructing the plan actuary to produce a plan valuation with a funding target 150 percent above the minimum dollar requirement, management realized that a host of means were available to the actuary to reduce ALPHA's desired funding goal from its current 167 percent of the minimum dollar requirement to 150 percent.[10] They also realized that the important decision—the 150 percent target—was theirs to make. By doing so in the manner described, they discharged their responsibilities, both as plan fiduciaries and as agents of the corporate shareholders.

The result is excellent plan member benefit payment security—including a reserve for future postretirement inflation updates. At the same time, shareholders also benefit from the healthy asset cushion. Much of it is available to help see ALPHA Corporation through periods of economic distress—should they occur. It also allows ALPHA's management to pursue a tax-deferred return-maximizing investment policy with pension plan assets.

Such a policy should pay off over the long term in terms of a low pension contribution rate. It would be difficult to pursue such a policy without a significant in-place asset cushion. Without it, a combination of poor shorter-term investment results and an ill-timed plan valuation could lead to an unplanned requirement to increase pension contributions at a possibly awkward time for the corporation.

However, in management's judgment the cushion size stops short of inviting demands for turning the cushion into unplanned benefit enhancements. It also stops short of eliciting accusations of tax avoidance from the tax authorities and of drawing the attention of asset raiders on the lookout for cashrich corporate victims.

Having decided on the size of ALPHA's pension fund, management turned its attention to determining the policies that would govern pension fund investments.

CHAPTER NOTES

1. See note 1, Chapter 2.
2. There are, of course, no hard and fast rules. The intricate arrays of methods and assumptions used to mathematically arrive at the funding target often get in the way of objectively studying what types of contingencies warrant what size of reserve—that is, asset cushion component. Such a study should also look at the covariance of

the contingencies. The more independent the contingencies, the smaller the total asset cushion required to assure payment of a given accrued pension liability.

The suggestion that the minimum asset cushion might be in the 20 percent range is only a guess. As ALPHA's consultants suggest later in the chapter, current regulations and regulator rules of thumb would likely accept a plan valuation with a 20 percent cushion implicit in it. This whole area would greatly benefit from further research—or, if the research has already been done somewhere, for it to be brought into the public domain so that it can be studied and discussed.

3. Current pension regulations in the United States permit a plan sponsor to effectively default on its pension obligations. Both assets and liabilities in that case are turned over to a government agency—the Pension Benefit Guaranty Corporation. If the PBGC deems there to be an asset shortfall—that is, a negative asset cushion relative to the plan wind-up liability—it can lay title to up to 30 percent of the sponsor's net worth.

If the size of negative asset cushion (e.g., the plan deficiency relative wind-up liabilities) exceeds 30 percent of the sponsor's net worth, such a transaction might well benefit the sponsor's shareholders at the expense of the PBGC—and, ultimately, the taxpayers. Rules vary by province in Canada. Ontario has a benefit insurance program that can claim up to 100 percent of the sponsor's net worth.

4. Business magazines such as *Business Week, Forbes,* and *Fortune* periodically write private pension system financial status stories using noncomparable funding targets (or actuarial liabilities) as a basis. Even the National Bureau Of Economic Research is guilty of this practice. Laurence Kotlikoff and Daniel Smith claim to be presenting the financial status of both private sector and public sector in their NBER-sponsored book *Pensions in the American Economy,* published by the University of Chicago Press, 1983.

This author reviewed the book in the Spring 1985 issue of *The Journal of Portfolio Management.* While praising its comprehensiveness and its presentation of heretofore virtually nonaccessible information on coverage and benefits in employer retirement systems, we found the financial status part of the book flawed. Assets and liabilities were simply not comparable between the private sector and public sector systems, or even within the sectors.

5. Discussions about immunization are often confusing. Discussants seldom clarify whether they are talking about an activity that follows from investment policy decisions or an activity that follows from a decision to release part of the existing pension plan asset cushion. At this point it is best understood as a formal technique for matching projected payment outgoes with principal and interest inflows from a bond portfolio "dedicated" to the matching exercise.

In theory such an exercise could be set up for both the fixed-dollar liabilities and the variable dollar liabilities. In practice, it has thus far only been applied to the fixed-dollar component for the simple reason that neither U.S. nor Canadian governments have yet seen fit to issue long-term inflation-linked bonds. All liabilities are fixed-dollar liabilities in career average and flat benefit plans. However, this is only true in a formal legal sense. Practically, through periodic benefit updates, the liabilities are in fact inflation-sensitive to a degree.

But, one might well ask, why bother going through this exercise without first addressing the big picture investment policy issues of asset mix policy and investment structure? The question is well posed. These issues should come first. Only after they have been addressed does immunization have a proper investment perspective from which it can be properly evaluated.

The reason many plan sponsors have been drawn to the technique is because of its asset cushion releasing power. With formally established immunization programs, actuaries will—with the authorities' blessing—use much higher return assumptions to discount fixed-dollar pension liabilities. However, Chapter Three showed that an asset cushion policy ought to be established first—independent of any consideration of how it might be implemented.

It also pointed out that there is a myriad of techniques—which can be used in an almost infinite variety of combinations—available to the actuary to justify a decided-on funding target. Immunization is only one such technique. Its use should only be considered if it is consistent with decided-on investment policy—especially asset mix policy.

6. ALPHA's use of an outside consultant to look at the financial side of its pension system is not unusual. Special skills—related to economics and capital markets, actuarial science, and law—are required. What might be a bit unusual is that we endow a single consulting organization with all these skills in this and subsequent chapters. Such one-stop shopping opportunities are rare in the pension finance consulting field. Often a marriage between an investment consultant and a benefits consultant must first be consummated. These marriages don't always work very well.

7. The return and inflation experience assumptions used in this particular analysis are reproduced in Table 3–4.

With these best estimate projections, the two minimum dollar requirements—without and with 60 percent CPI protection after retirement—can be estimated. These requirements can then be compared with the funding target that resulted from the use of much lower actuarial projections used in the most recent actuarial valuation. These estimates are shown in Figure 3–5 in the chapter.

8. Actuarial funding methods, fully described and mathematically derived, can (and do) fill books all by themselves. The simplest and most intuitively obvious method is to each year set aside an amount that will pay for the benefit earned that year. This is the unit credit or single premium method.

This method is sometimes falsely accused of automatically leading to progressively higher contribution rates over time. Such an accusation confuses the funding dynamics of this method for a single individual with those for a group of individuals. For an individual, contributions must rise as retirement approaches: there is less and less time for the contributions to earn investment income to help pay for benefits that are probably rising if they are based on final earnings. For a group, however, as plan members retire they are replaced by new entrants with many contribution years ahead of them. Consequently, for the group, the contribution rate only rises if the average age of the group rises.

TABLE 3–4 Return and Inflation Experience Assumptions

	Consultant's Best Estimates		Used in Most Recent Actuarial Valuation
	Near Term	Far Term	
Return	12%	8%	6%
Wages	9	6 1/2	4 1/2
Prices	8	5	N/A

Other funding methods generally build up an asset cushion component that could be used to keep the contribution rate constant even in the event the average age of the group rises. Consequently, they lead—*centeris paribus*—to higher funding targets than the unit credit method.

The other dimension of funding methods deals with what to do in case an actuarial valuation produces a result where plan assets—not necessarily at market—are smaller or greater than the funding target. Basically, in this case the "surplus" or "deficiency" can be amortized quickly—indeed, immediately under certain circumstances—or very slowly—15 years or more under certain circumstances.

We mentioned in note 5 that the actuary had an army of tools available to justify a chosen funding target. Funding methods, along with immunization, return assumptions, inflation assumptions, and a host of work force demographics-related assumptions are part of that army.

9. Accountants have been studying the treatment of pensions on plan sponsor balance sheets and profit and loss statements for over a decade now. One important result of these studies is *FASB 35,* issued in March 1980. It sets out the accounting standards for defined benefit pension plans. Two of its features are especially noteworthy. Assets are to be stated at market—book values or various types of smoothed values are not acceptable. Liabilities are to be stated using "realistic" return assumptions as the discount rate. In other words, accountants want what we call the minimum dollar requirement in the chapter.

A controversial feature of *FASB 35* is that, in the case of final earnings plans, no salary projection is required in calculating the minimum dollar requirement. In Chapter Three we suggest that for financial planning purposes such a projection should be made before the accrued pension debt is calculated. It strikes us as inconsistent to use discount rates that contain an inflation premium but not to recognize the same inflation phenomenon in estimating what benefits, as stated in the plan text, will actually have to be paid.

Despite this possible shortcoming—debatable, we admit—*FASB 35* is an important step toward uniformity in financial reporting of defined benefit pension plans. McGill's comments on *FASB 35* (in *Fundamentals of Private Pensions*) from the actuarial community's perspective are illuminating:

"*FASB 35* values may differ substantially from those developed for other purposes . . . The uninitiated may be confused by the discrepancies between the two balance sheets [i.e., the actuarial and the *FASB 35* balance sheets] . . . Many actuaries and others question the value of the *FASB 35* exercise."

We wonder how accountants feel about the value of the actuarial balance sheet creation exercise!

FASB 36 requires that the key elements of *FASB 35* be disclosed in footnotes to the plan sponsor financial statements. On the question of the disclosure of annual pension costs, FASB philosophy focuses on estimating expenses as they accrue rather than on recording actual sponsor contributions when made. As we have seen, actual contributions could in any year be significantly more or less than the actual pension expense incurred in that year.

10. Chapter Three discussion has alluded to a number of these means. They include asset valuation methods, accrued benefit estimation methods, funding methods, and a host of possible plan experience assumptions. These assumptions can relate to anything ranging from quit rate, retirement age, and mortality experience to such economic assumptions as investment return and price and wage inflation. All these means are at hand to create large, medium-sized, or small asset cushion targets in defined benefit plans.

CHAPTER FOUR

Asset Mix Policy: How Should the Pension Plan's Capital Be Deployed?

A man surprised is half beaten.

—Old English Proverb

There are two policy extremes. The risk-minimizing policy avoids surprises but is likely to be very expensive for shareholders over the long haul. The return-maximizing policy, on the other hand, is likely to be the most cost-effective policy for shareholders over the long haul; however, it involves potentially large swings in fund market value over the shorter term.

This chapter explores these good news–bad news extremes and how a reasonable compromise between the two may be struck. It also makes an important distinction between types of asset mix decisions.

The policy decision—deciding on the most appropriate long-term/short-term risk/return trade-off—and asset mix shift decision—deciding on if and how to move away from the policy asset mix—are very different decisions. Plan sponsors and money managers that fail to distinguish between them will not make either decision well.

WHAT IS ASSET MIX POLICY?

Asset mix policy reflects the pension plan sponsor's intentions regarding the structure of the asset side of the pension plan balance sheet. Using

53

the words introduced in Chapter Two, policy alternatives can range from being value-maximizing at one extreme to risk-minimizing at the other. The value and the risk of what? Ultimately, the focus for value maximization or risk minimization must be the plan asset cushion. This cushion is the economic link between the plan and its sponsor. The larger the cushion's value, the larger economic value of the sponsor, and vice versa.

Given a benefits policy that defines the liabilities and a funding policy that determines the net cash flow into or out of the pension system, the connection between the asset cushion and asset mix policy is obvious. A value-maximizing asset mix policy attempts to grow the asset cushion as rapidly as possible. A risk-minimizing asset mix policy attempts to maximize the predictability and stability of the asset cushion. Thus, it minimizes the likelihood the cushion will ever totally disappear.

Having stated what it is, it is as important to state what asset mix policy is not. It does not encompass decisions to temporarily shift the actual asset mix away from the policy mix. Such decisions are as much investment decisions as are decisions to buy or sell individual securities. They will be discussed in the investment management related chapters.

However, there is an obvious connection between asset mix policy and shifts around the resulting policy asset mix: what size shifts should be permitted? Just as good shifts will enhance total fund return, so will bad shifts detract from it. Asset mix policy sets out the basic risk posture for the corporation's pension assets. Consequently, the degree to which asset mix shifts are permitted to impact the overall pension system risk position is an asset mix policy issue.

The Risk-Minimizing Asset Mix Policy

The search for the most suitable policy for a specific fund is sometimes initiated by instructing a computer to simulate possible financial outcomes using every asset mix conceivable over the full range of return and inflation possibilities. This often results in pounds of computer printouts, large consulting fees, and no new insights into asset mix policy.

It is much better to start by focusing on one policy only and then to see if it can be improved on. The natural policy to examine first is the one that minimizes the corporation's overall risk exposure to its pension operation. An outline of this policy has already been presented in Chapter Two. It had three basic characteristics. First, this policy attempts as closely as possible to match the length and inflation-sensitivity of the accrued pension obligations. Second, it does not undertake any credit or equity risk. Third, the resulting asset mix policy is passively imple-

FIGURE 4-1   The Risk-Minimizing Asset Mix Policy

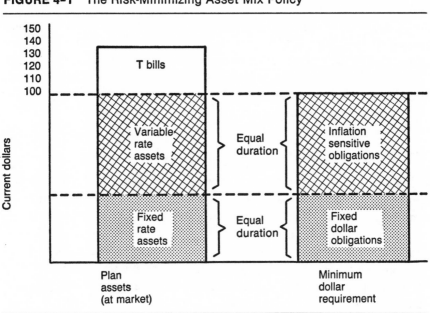

mented—that is, no attempt is made to make money by outsmarting other investors.

Figure 4-1 reproduces the graphical representation of the risk-minimizing asset mix policy of Chapter Two. Note that the liabilities are split into fixed and variable dollar components so that they can be properly matched with like assets. The asset cushion is invested in T-bills.

The logic of this policy is straightforward. There are typically two types of accrued pension obligations in an employer pension plan. First, there are the obligations to plan members who are no longer active employees—mainly pensioners. Despite some notable exceptions, most plan texts state these obligations to be fixed in dollar terms—typically involving a regular monthly sum to be paid until the recipient dies. Second, there are obligations to active employees. These are usually tied to earnings during the employees' best years—usually their final years—after which the obligations are paid out as a lump sum or become fixed-dollar obligations as the employees terminate or retire.

A matching investment policy dictates the establishment of a securities portfolio where the cash inflows match the cash outflows—ideally exactly. For the typical pension plan this means having fixed and variable dollar asset components, proportionate to the relative sizes of the accrued obligations.

Ensuring the expected asset-related payments will indeed be made when due suggests holding the debt securities of the highest quality credits only. The safest investment avenue for the surplus assets—that is, assets in excess of those needed to match fixed and variable dollar obligations—would seem to be T-bills. They have no credit risk, they are very liquid, and their yields have tracked inflation very well.

Implementing a Risk-Minimizing Asset Mix Policy

This policy is more than just an interesting concept. It can actually be implemented if a corporation decides it best suits its particular situation and/or philosophy. The advent of stripping the coupons from the traditional bond (with its traditional string of six-month interest coupons) has greatly facilitated matching fixed-dollar outgoes and inflows. With the reinvestment rate problem associated with the traditional bond so eliminated, the mechanics of actually matching payments have become quite simple.

Even without exact payment matching, duration matching provides a close substitute. With the duration—that is, the payment present value-weighted average length—of the fixed-dollar pension payment obligations easily within reach of the duration of standard long government bonds, duration matching is also a totally feasible strategy.[1]

The ideal bond for matching the wage inflation-related pension obligations would be default-free, inflation-indexed, and very long. Such vehicles do not exist in North American capital markets, although they do in Great Britain. The closest practical alternative in the United States and Canada is probably the federal government T-bill. It is default-free, and it can be rolled over into the next issue every three or six months.[2]

Thus the T-bill offers no long-term guarantee of an inflation-indexed rate of return. But because short-term interest rates have followed the inflation rate reasonably closely, the T-bill has been a good inflation hedge. In a free capital market, it is likely to remain a good inflation hedge.

The Problem with the Risk-Minimizing Asset Mix Policy

Simply put, the problem is expense. Some simple arithmetic can demonstrate this. An often-used rule of thumb in relating pension fund return and pension cost is that a 1 percentage point swing in long-term return can be equivalent to a 25 percent swing in the cost of providing a given pension.

Relate this rule now to the historical observation and reasonable prospective expectation that the return on equity investments has been and should be considerably higher—by as much as 5 or more percent—than the return on T-bills. The conclusion is obvious. Over the long run, a pension system secured by a fund mainly in T-bills could be as much as twice or three times as expensive—in terms of the corporate contribution rate required to support it—as one secured by an all-equity fund.

Possibly, then, the next stop in the search for the right asset mix policy should be an all-equity policy. If it has produced and should continue to produce the lowest cost pension system over the long haul for the corporation, why not adopt it?

The Problem with the Return-Maximizing Asset Mix Policy

The problem here is the discontinuity of corporate events. If the corporation and its pension system were truly impervious to the passage of time with no one caring about the possible financial status of the system at a particular point in time, an all-equity policy could well be argued to be riskless—and the realized equity premium a gift from less fortunate capital market participants.

Of course, corporations are subject to discontinuities. Their main businesses are subject to the vagaries of their own market places—leading to changes in ability to make pension contributions. Yet the pension plan must be subjected to an actuarial evaluation at least once every three years. Such evaluations would uncover poor investment experience if it occurred and could dictate higher contribution requirements at inopportune times.

Corporations exist under the watchful eyes of financial analysts who attempt to find differences between the intrinsic value and market value of their shares. If they are doing their job properly, analysts would take into account changes in the aftertax value of the asset cushion in the pension plan.

Finally, there is the finite career span of corporate managers themselves. It is human nature to attempt to accomplish measurable goals not just within careers, but within subcareers, postings, and even temporary assignments.

All these considerations point in the direction of shorter-term fluctuations in the value of the pension fund being a matter of some consequence. Of how much consequence? The next few sections of this chapter will suggest how this question might be answered.

Shorter-Term Pension Fund Value Fluctuations: How Much Consequence?

There are at least two sets of calculations worth making to help answer this question. Even if the pension system is viewed as an entity segregated from the main business, the contribution rate connection inevitably remains. In establishing the pension fund risk policy, managers should have an idea as to what range of future contribution rates it might lead to. Viewed on a more integrated basis, the risk policy focus shifts to the future fate of the asset cushion—a legitimate, although pretax, corporate asset for most corporations.

In both types of analyses there is a trade-off to be made, typically between good news in the long run—the next 20 years or more—and the possibility of bad news in the shorter run—the next three to five years or so. Figure 4–2 depicts these trade-offs visually.

Actually deciding where longer-term gain and shorter-term pain balance each other requires that some numbers be placed in the boxes on the weigh scales. It would be foolish to pretend these numbers have a high degree of accuracy attached to them. In this age of discontinuity, the future that will unfold is not easy to discern.

The long-term economic numbers below are from the same best estimate family that we philosophized about in Chapter Two (see especially note[3]) and used to estimate the best estimate liabilities in Chapter Three. They should represent our best effort to blend history and com-

FIGURE 4-2 The Good News–Bad News Trade-Offs

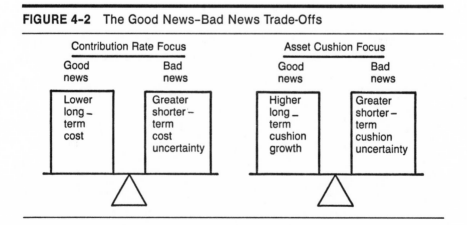

mon sense with the faith that is required to make the unavoidable leap into an unknown future.

A likely result is the postulation of real returns on equity-oriented investments from possibly 3 to 7 percent and up, with the low end of the risk scale represented by a well-diversified portfolio of zero-leverage, high-quality real estate and the high end represented by small capitalization common stocks and venture capital. Real returns on debt investments might range from 1 to 4 percent, with T-bills at the low end of the risk scale and lower-grade, long-term bonds at the high end. These ranges are consistent with both history and logic and were used in Figure 2–5 in Chapter Two. Figure 4–3 reproduces the asset mix policy components of the overall investment policy real return targets first introduced in Figure 2–5.

While no more or less important than the long-term numbers, the development of a set of three to five-year numbers requires somewhat more work. A single set of best estimates suffers from the inability to shed any light on the question of risk, the very reason for performing the shorter-term analysis. The recognition of more than one outcome is now essential. However, it is equally true that the recognition of too many can easily lead to information overload for the decision makers.

FIGURE 4-3   Asset Mix Policy and Long-Term Return Targets

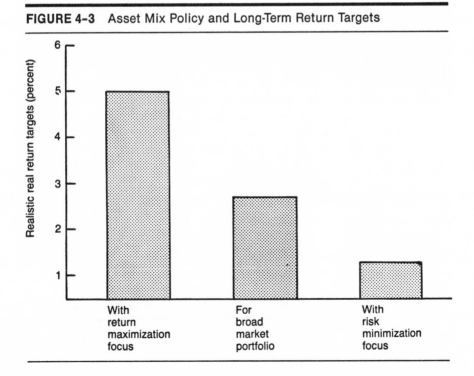

TABLE 4-1 Possible Three-to Five-Year Capital Market Environments

The Environment	*The Capital Markets*
Good Times: steady output and productivity growth, low inflation rate, positive expectations about the future.	Stocks do very well, followed by real estate and long bonds. Short-term investments left far behind.
Stagflation: uneven output and productivity growth, inflation rate in the 6–9 percent range, confused expectations about the future.	No predictable differences in asset class returns.
Rising Inflation: uneven output and productivity growth, debt monetization, inflation rate rising above 10 percent, dynamics expected to continue.	Real estate and other tangibles do best, stocks and short-term investments mediocre, long bonds worse by far.
Deflation: output stagnant to falling, inflation low and falling, future looks bleak.	High-quality long bonds best by far, cash mediocre, real estate poor, stocks worst.

An effective compromise is to develop a limited number of credible capital market environments that could actually occur over the next three to five years. Four that might do the job are shown in Table 4-1.[3]

There are at least two benefits to this approach of dealing with an unknown future. First, historical experience can now be used in a much more focused way. Rather than just asking what stocks or bonds have done in the past, it is much more instructive to ask how they performed in an environment with a set of specific socioeconomic characteristics. Related to this question is an even more challenging one: What are today's pricing relationships in relation to those at the start of the historical period?[4]

The second benefit is that the approach explicitly deals with the likely interrelationships between the returns of the various capital market components among themselves and with inflation. Effective risk control means finding the cheapest possible insurance[5] against undesirable events. In an asset mix policy context, this means having some idea what for example, stocks might be doing if bonds don't do well, and vice versa.

Once all the needed long- and shorter-term economic judgments have been expressed numerically, a financial model of the pension system can be employed to see what kind of future contribution rate and as-

FIGURE 4-4   The Future Contribution Rate Trade-off Range

The Return Maximizing Policy		The Risk Minimizing Policy
Good news	Bad news	No good or bad news
Long – term contributions are 6% of payroll	Shorter – term contributions could be over 15% of payroll in deflation	Contributions will not vary far from 10% of payroll in short term or long term

set cushion value ranges the risk-minimizing and return-maximizing asset mix policies could produce.

Such a model need not be particularly high-powered—and therefore complicated and expensive. There is little sense in being extremely precise in making financial projections into a future that is only dimly seen and is being represented by numbers conveying orders of magnitude rather than exactness.

What the model should do is to convert those numeric impressions into financial orders of magnitude of the good news–bad news trade-offs facing management in the pension system. Using the weigh scales once more, they now display what might be typical[6] trade-offs in a final average plan where the current asset cushion is also the target asset cushion. Figure 4-4 displays them in terms of possible contribution rates three to five years hence.

Similarly, the trade-off range can be expressed in asset cushion terms. This is done in Figure 4-5.

The weigh scales have only depicted the two most extreme of asset mix policy choices. Between the return-maximizing and risk-minimizing policies lies the full in-between spectrum. Judging by the asset mix policies actually being pursued[7] by corporate pension funds, it is somewhere in between that most managements prefer to be—either through an explicitly analyzed choice, or by simply following the safety-in-numbers principle: if everybody else is doing it, why be different?

FIGURE 4-5 The Future Asset Cushion Trade-off Range

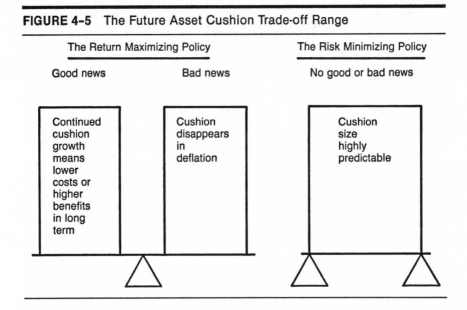

Before we return to the executive offices of ALPHA Corporation, there are two more important issues to review: the asset mix shift issue and an issue that has recently received considerable attention—although thus far mainly in academic circles—the tax arbitrage issue.

The Asset Mix Shift Issue

There is nothing wrong with maintaining an unchanging policy asset mix through significant fluctuations in capital market prices. Indeed, such a "steady helm" approach would automatically force moving cash flow in the direction of the relatively poorest performing asset class—and away from the best performing one—and so would produce the benefits of dollar averaging for the fund.

However, this approach runs counter to the action-oriented philosophy often an integral part of corporate culture. Such a philosophy demands that capital market fluctuations be "worked" to the advantage of the fund. This demand in turn often leads to serious flaws in the pension fund investment program: confusion between the basic asset mix policy, temporary shifts away from it, and questions over who is responsible for what.

To avoid these flaws, corporate management must understand that asset mix shift decisions cannot be made through the same decision process just described for making asset mix policy decisions. Successful as-

---

TABLE 4-2   Five Steps to Setting up a Successful Shift Program

---

Step 1   Recognize that the asset mix shift program should be set up as a separate component of the overall fund program.

Step 2   Decide the size of the shift program as a percentage of the overall fund. A quantitatively refined approach would involve making assumptions about the predictive accuracy of successful market timers—discounted by the predictive accuracy of the search process that tries to identify one or more of them—and then relating the resulting incremental- return/ incremental-risk parameters to the basic return/risk parameters implicit in the original policy asset mix decision.[8] Possibly more practical, the following rule of thumb may be applied: anything much less than 10 percent of the fund is probably tokenism; anything over 30 percent is probably too risky.

Step 3   Fund the asset mix shift account explicitly by assigning portions of the already decided-on asset class policy weights to it. For example, if the bond and stock policy weights are 50 percent each, a 20 percent shift account could be established by taking 10 percent each from the policy bond and stock money. This formal funding process establishes a benchmark portfolio against which a value-added target can be set.

Step 4   Set a realistic value-added target in relation to a benchmark portfolio funded from the asset mix policy weights. Annual excess return of 3 percent in relation to the benchmark portfolio would be a demanding but not unrealistic target—more on this in Chapter Five.

Step 5   Initiate a search process that maximizes the chances that the manager(s) selected will be able to hit the target—more on this in Chapter Six.

---

set shifters are an exotic subset of the value-added branch of the investment management community. If the pension fund is to be subjected to this investment management dimension, the actual buy-sell decisions are ideally made by one or more of these specialists—more on this in later chapters.

Asset shift management, however, cannot exist in a vacuum. It must be connected to and consistent with asset mix policy decisions. Obviously, it should only be pursued if it is expected to improve the basic good news–bad news trade-off already decided on through the policy asset mix decision.

In the final analysis, such a judgment is an act of faith. It must rest on the belief that the prospects for incremental fund return created justify not only the incremental risks asset mix shifting entails with a skilled asset mix shifter, but also the risk that the asset mix shifter turns out to be less skilled than hoped. Despite the need for an act of faith, some concrete actions can be taken to maximize the chances of success for an asset mix shift program.

The Tax Arbitrage Issue

This issue is grounded in the fact that investment income and capital gains are tax-exempt inside a pension fund. In the corporation's hands, however, returns on equity investments are subject to a much lower rate of taxation than returns on debt investments. By contrast, dividend payments by the corporation are not expenses for tax purposes, while interest payments are.

This combination of facts creates the opportunity to possibly lower taxes payable for the corporation. It can be exploited without any change in the combined capital structure of the firm and its defined benefit pension plan. All that is required for its execution is to have a pension fund asset mix policy that includes at least some equity investments, to be able to issue corporate bonds on reasonable financial terms, and to have corporate income subject to taxation.

In that situation aftertax income can be increased by moving the pension fund equity investments onto the corporate balance sheet—leaving its return still subject to a zero or at most low tax rate—issuing an equivalent dollar amount of corporate bonds—with their interest cost reducing taxable income—and using the proceeds to acquire an equivalent bond position in the pension fund where its return is tax-sheltered. The bond position acquired is equivalent to the bonds issued in amount, term, and, ideally, yield. However, the bonds acquired are *not* the bonds issued. This "swap" is further explored in the Chapter Notes.[9]

It is worth reflecting on a remarkable contrast between this tax arbitrage issue and the asset mix shift issue. The former technique appears to offer a much surer path to increasing aftertax profit than the latter. Yet virtually all pension funds are subjected to some form of asset mix shift management—although often with little vigor and conviction.

By contrast, tax arbitrage has not even reached the discussion stage on most executive floors. When it does, implementation is by no means guaranteed: the technique would make fluctuations in the equity portfolio much more visible to the public eye, could significantly change the appearance of the main business balance sheet, and, if implemented widely enough, could trigger a review of the whole area by the tax authorities.

AN ASSET MIX POLICY FOR ALPHA CORPORATION

As ALPHA's management prepared itself for the task of establishing a formal asset mix policy for its pension fund, it reread its responses to the questions on the investment policy questionnaire used to write the statement of purposes and goals for the fund (see Table 4-3).

The responses point very clearly to the return-maximizing end of the asset mix policy spectrum. Realizing the need for some analytical work before a specific decision could be made, the consultant[10] was engaged with a mandate which is summarized in Table 4-4.

TABLE 4-3   Investment Policy Questionnaire: ALPHA Corporation's Responses

---

Asset Cushion Ownership
Can we make decisions assuming the corporation owns all or most of the asset cushion? Y/N
"Yes."

Minimum Risk Policy
Do we know the zero-default risk asset mix that best matches the length and inflation-sensitivity of our pension obligations at this time? Y/N
"Yes, this portfolio would have 15 percent in long-term, default-free, fixed-rate bonds, 55 percent in long-term, default-free, variable rate bonds, and the rest in T-bills."

Current Asset Cushion
Do we have a recent estimate of our actual asset cushion? Y/N
"Yes, it is $400 million or 30 percent of assets."

Asset Mix Policy
Are we prepared to take on default and equity risk in the fund in order to improve its return prospects? Y/N
"Yes, we believe our pension system and the corporation behind it have the financial strength to undertake such risk without endangering the benefit promises made."
If Y, some of this type of risk or a lot?
"As much as can be taken without reducing the asset cushion below the minimum required level as determined by the actuary."

Investment Management
Do we believe active management can add value? Y/N
"Yes."
Do we believe that we can identify active managers who will be successful—before, rather than after the fact?
"We are by no means certain we can. However, we are willing to take some calculated risks here. The fund's exposure to active management will be carefully controlled and monitored."

TABLE 4-4 The Consultant's Mandate

Economic Assumptions: Suggest a set of reasonable long-term real return assumptions for stocks, real estate, long bonds, and T-bills. Suggest sets of reasonable nominal return and inflation assumptions for three-to-five year timeframes that could be characterized by the descriptions *good times, stagflation, rising inflation,* and *deflation,* respectively.

Long-Term Plan Costs: Using existing benefit formulas and assuming constant work force characteristics, estimate what the long-term real rate projections imply for long-term normal plan costs. In making these calculations, also assume a long-term inflation rate of 6 percent and that we will continue our habitual practice of adjusting pensions in pay for 60 percent of CPI increases.

Shorter-Term Contribution Rates: Keeping all existing actuarial methods and assumptions constant, estimate what the sixth-year contribution rate would be in each of the four postulated capital market environments for three policy asset mixes. Do this for the return-maximizing policy, the risk-minimizing policy, and the return-maximizing policy that also keep the sixth-year contribution rate below 10 percent of payroll in all four environments.

Shorter-Term Asset Cushion Swings: Estimate what might happen to the current $400 million asset cushion in the same context for the same three policies.

The Asset Mix Shift Issue: Recommend how we should proceed on this issue.

The Tax Arbitrage Issue: Explain the relevance of this issue to ALPHA and tell us what our options are.

Four weeks later the consultants were back with their report. As requested, they dealt with all of the mandate items in turn.

Consultant's Report: Long-Term Plan Costs

The consultants produced a table expressing their views on reasonable real return assumptions and their calculations of the resulting normal plan costs under the conditions set out in ALPHA's Consultant's Mandate. The Table 4-5 suggests that the plan conforms to the rough 1:25 rule. A 1 percentage point swing in real return results in an approximate 20 percent to 30 percent swing in normal plan cost. Given this rule and the suggestion that a 5 percentage point return differential between the highest and lowest risk classes is a realistic long-term assumption, the "why not 100% stocks?" question is very much brought to the fore.

TABLE 4–5 Long-Term Economic Assumptions and Normal Plan Costs

Asset Class	Long-Term Real Return	Long-Term Normal Cost (percent of payroll)
Stocks	5%	6%
Real estate	4	7
Long bonds	2	10
T-bills	.5	14

Consultant's Report: Shorter-Term Contribution Rate Swings

The consultant's table (Table 4–6 below) on possible contribution rates six years hence turned out to be equally instructive. The return-maximizing policy's shorter-term good and bad news range was extreme, while the risk-minimizing policy produced a very narrow outcome range. The latter contribution range came in below the long-term normal cost projection by a considerable margin.

Recall, however, that the long-term numbers include 60 percent CPI indexation while the shorter-term numbers—mirroring the actuary's methods—do not. In addition, the consultant's numbers reflected a current contribution rate 2 1/2 percentage points above the normal cost rate and a view that real interest rates would be somewhat higher in the shorter term.

The table suggests that there is insurance against the return-maximizing bad news outcome available at what appears to be reasonable cost. The numbers represent the company contribution rate ex-

TABLE 4–6 Sixth-Year Contribution Rate Projections

	Return Maximization with Bad News	Return Maximization No Bad News	Risk Minimization
Good times	– 14%	– 10%	4%
Stagflation	8	7	6
Rising inflation	7	8	8
Deflation	18	9	4

FIGURE 4-6 Sixth-Year Contribution Rate Projections

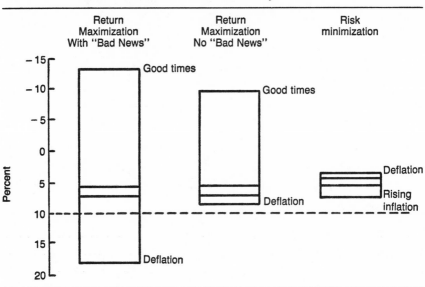

pressed as a percentage of payroll. Actuarial gains and losses are being amortized over a 15-year basis.

A negative value in the table represents good news. It means a large enough surplus is being recognized that, if amortized over 15 years, it would exceed the normal cost, leading—if only hypothetically—to negative corporate contributions, at least in the sixth year from now.

These results were also presented graphically in relation to the expressed maximum acceptable contribution rate. The scale in Figure 4–6 is the contribution rate expressed as a percentage of payroll. The line drawn at 10 percent represents the bad news line.

Consultant's Report: Shorter-Term Asset Cushion Swings

ALPHA's management was aware from the financial status work previously performed that the pension plan is in good financial shape. Against assets at market of $1.3 billion, accrued best estimate plan obligations are $0.9 to $1.1 billion, depending on whether the traditional inflation updates to pensioners are treated as a formal obligation.

The consultant realized that the client wanted an assessment of what impact a chosen asset mix policy might have three to five years hence on the $200–$400 million cushion value. Recognizing that the ac-

FIGURE 4-7   Five-Year Asset Cushion Swing Projections

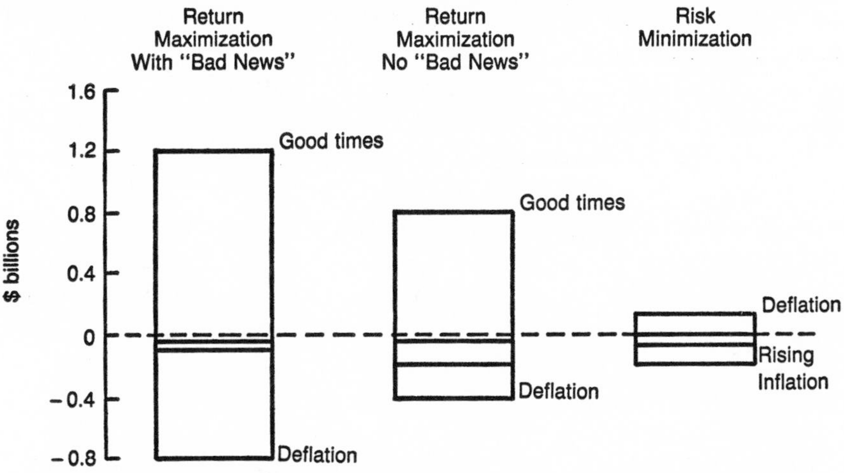

crued obligation was calculated assuming a real rate of return in the 3 percent area, it followed that if the current $1.3 billion fund grew to $1.5 billion in today's dollars in five years—that is, at a real rate of 3 percent—the current financial status of the plan should approximately stay intact.

Actual asset values—in today's dollars in five years—could be calculated using the three-policy asset mixes already identified and the scenario-based capital market and inflation projections. The difference between these asset values and the $1.5 billion benchmark value should provide a good approximation of the potential impact a particular mix might have on increasing or decreasing today's $200–$400 million asset cushion. The resulting asset cushion swing estimates are presented in Figure 4–7. They are denominated in billions of dollars.

Note that the return-maximizing and risk-minimizing policies show their now expected characteristics quite dramatically in asset cushion swing dollars. The latter policy's swings are small; the former's large— in the $1.2 billion dollar area in Good times (increase) and the $0.8 billion area in Deflation (decrease).

The policy previously identified as return-maximizing, but with the constraint of keeping the corporate contribution rate below 10 percent of payroll six years hence, offers $400 million of deflation protection at a cost of giving up part of the large cushion gain projected for Good times.[11]

The Consultant's Policy Asset Mix Recommendation

The middle asset mix in the displays seems capable of providing AL-PHA Corporation with the most acceptable blend of long-term return maximization prospects and shorter-term defensive characteristics. It was found by the consultant through tests that focused on keeping the sixth-year contribution rate under 10 percent of payroll. Its basic structure is 75 percent equity investments—25 percent debt investments. This mix is consistent with a long-term real return target of 4 percent.

The equity component breaks down into a 50 percent stock component and a 25 percent real estate component. The 50 percent stock content provides the nucleus of the fund's high long-term earning power prospects, buttressed by a 25 percent position in commercial real estate, which should do especially well should rising inflation best describe the next three to five years.[12]

Placing the rest of the fund in high-quality long (the longer the better) bonds controls its downside exposure to a prolonged period of little or no real economic growth. It does so well enough to—should a *deflation*-like period occur—permit ALPHA to continue sponsoring the current plan without a dramatic rise in the contribution rate.

In deploying the 50 percent stock position, at least two considerations deserve attention at the policy level. There has been a marked tendency among pension funds to invest the stock money in quality, larger capitalization stocks with long track records and with company head offices in our own country. This tendency ignores two other stock investment areas with considerable profit and diversification potential.

First, close to 50 percent of the market value of companies large enough to be listed on stock exchanges do not have their head offices in North America. While there are reasons justifying their underrepresentation on a capitalization basis, there are no reasons why they should have zero representation.[13]

Second, while the small business sector of our national economy is dwarfed in capitalization by the large business sector, it should not be ignored by pension funds. A well-diversified and professionally managed small company portfolio provides the dual benefits of potentially higher longer-term return to pension funds and of providing patient risk capital to the entrepreneurial sector of the economy.[14]

Reasonable target weightings are 10 percent to 20 percent for foreign investments and 5 percent to 10 percent for small business investments, leaving 20 percent to 35 percent for domestic larger capitalization stocks. The actual implementation of investment programs in both the foreign and domestic small business areas should be carried out by specialists in those respective fields.

The Asset Mix Shift Recommendation

It is consistent with ALPHA's action-oriented corporate culture that a mechanism exists for altering the actual asset mix based on anticipated capital market movements. However, the operation of this mechanism should not be confused with establishing asset mix policy. A segregated asset mix shift account should be established.

At a size of 20 percent of the total fund, such an account would be large enough that good performance would result in a measurable contribution to total fund results but not so large that poor results would seriously undermine the intent of the underlying policy asset mix. The major risk with implementing this recommendation is not fund exposure to down-side disaster—the 20 percent size limitation takes care of that. Instead, it is selection risk. There is no guarantee that the market timing specialist(s) selected will actually deliver longer-term incremental fund return. If they don't, extra fees, extra transaction costs, and extra risk will have been incurred for no gain.

Funding the account with 10 percent each of the policy stock and bond weights would create a 50-50 stock-bond index benchmark for the account. For the account to justify its existence, a value-added target in the 3 percent per annum area should be set. The account should be managed by professionals psychologically attuned to manage money aggressively with a market timing focus.

The Tax Arbitrage Recommendation

Had the recommended asset mix policy been in force last year, ALPHA's $70 million tax bill could have been halved. To have actually achieved this, however, would have required carrying the recommended $700 million stock and $350 million real estate positions on the corporate balance sheet and issuing $1,050 million of new ALPHA bonds. Clearly, such seemingly dramatic corporate balance sheet moves would have attracted widespread attention.

This whole area should be put out for study to ALPHA's financial and tax advisors. They should be advised to take the matter up with the tax authorities on a no-name basis before reporting back with their findings.

ALPHA's Decisions

ALPHA's management judged that the consultants' work was thorough and that their recommendations reflected both the corporation's culture and aspirations and the current realities of the pension plan's and ALPHA's financial condition. Consequently, ALPHA decided to adopt the

FIGURE 4-8 ALPHA Corporation's Asset Mix Policy

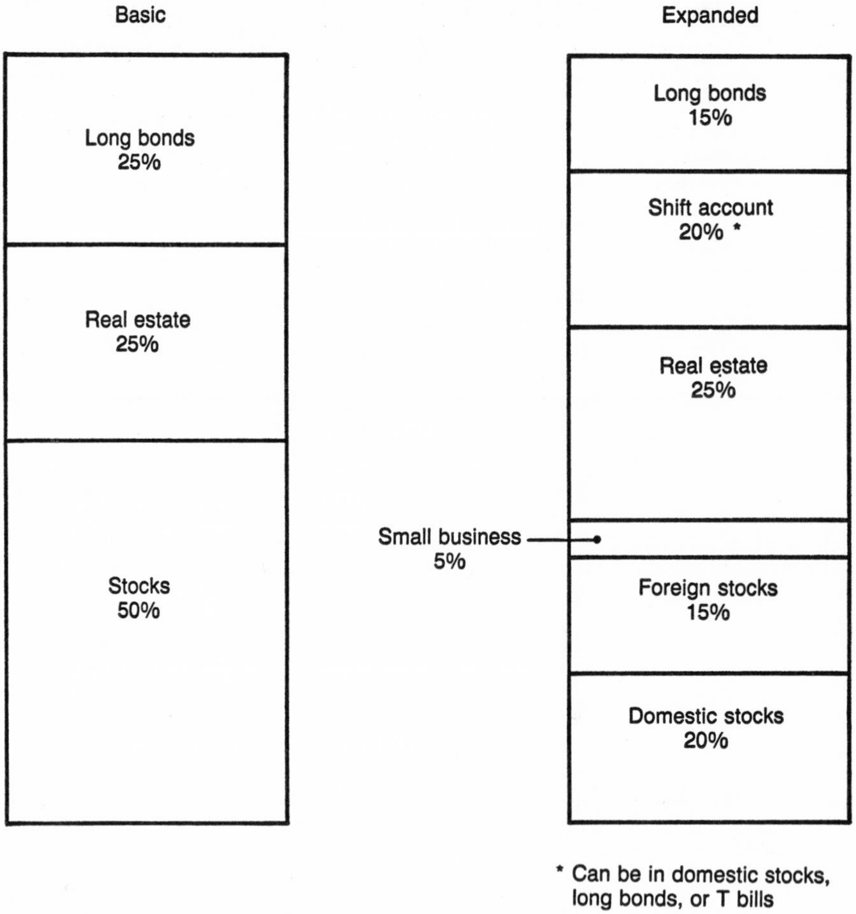

Basic

| Long bonds 25% |
| Real estate 25% |
| Stocks 50% |

Expanded

| Long bonds 15% |
| Shift account 20% * |
| Real estate 25% |
| Foreign stocks 15% |
| Domestic stocks 20% |

Small business — 5%

* Can be in domestic stocks, long bonds, or T bills

consultants' recommendations as its own and to take them to its board of directors—specifically, its pension investment committee—for approval.

There, with only a modest amount of discussion, was ALPHA Corporation's pension fund asset mix policy approved with only one caveat. The approval was subject to all aspects of the policy being implementable through ALPHA's investment management structure in a fiduciarily responsible manner.

The basic three-asset class policy of stocks, real estate, and bonds is shown first in Figure 4–8. It is then expanded to include the other recommended policy dimensions of foreign and small business investments and of the asset mix shift account. Thus, out of the original 25 percent long bond position, 15 percentage points remain permanently in long bonds. The other 10 percentage points have been transferred into the shift account.

Out of the original 50 percent stocks position, 20 percentage points go to domestic stocks, 15 to foreign stocks, 5 to small business. Again, the remaining 10 percentage points have been transferred into the shift account.

With asset mix policy decided, an important part of investment policy for the pension subsidiary is in place. The other important part of investment policy is deciding on how the asset mix policy is to be implemented through an investment management structure. It is to this question that ALPHA's management turns next.

CHAPTER NOTES

1. The concept of immunization was first introduced in Chapter Three. We suggested there the importance of distinguishing between using immunization to release part of the asset cushion and using it as part of a decided-on asset mix policy. Now we see it as part of implementing a low-risk asset mix policy. Literature on various immunization techniques—dedication, duration matching, etc.—abounds in such publications as the *Journal of Portfolio Management* and the *Financial Analysts Journal*. Whatever the specific technique, the general idea is to immunize portfolio return against interest rate risk. See note 2 below for a specific reference.

2. The article, "Real Immunization with Indexed Bonds" by David Babbel, *Financial Analysts Journal,* November–December 1984, contrasts nominal return with real return immunization. Canada's minister of finance has asked the Canadian financial community to comment on the advisability of the Canadian government issuing long, inflation-linked bonds.

3. This author's November–December 1977 *Financial Analysts Journal* article U.S. "Stock Prices and Interest Rates: A Three-to-Five-Year View" was one of the first, if not the first, to suggest that the scenario approach can be a very powerful tool in an investment planning context. Since then, the concept has been revisited by Michael Edesess and George Hambrecht in "Scenario Forecasting: Necessity, Not Choice," *Journal of Portfolio Management,* Spring 1980, and by Peter Carman, "The Trouble with Asset Allocation," *Journal of Portfolio Management,* Fall 1981. The *JPM*'s editor, Peter Bernstein, looks at the future regularly through scenarios in his own forecasting work.

4. In commenting on this chapter, Peter Bernstein emphasized the importance of how well investors anticipate a certain investment scenario as a determinant of what returns the scenario actually produces. Extreme good news and bad news capital market returns and the events that caused them are, almost by definition, unanticipated by the majority of investors.

5. Diversification can be a cost-effective way of buying insurance, depending on the amount of expected return forgone. Note that this chapter focuses on insurance against two types of bad news events: higher contribution rates and asset cushion declines three to five years hence.

Sophisticated methods titled "dynamic asset allocation" have been devised to ensure that a prespecified shorter-term nominal return is assured of being earned as a minimum. While these techniques produce the promised results, they only do so at a cost in longer-term fund return forgone. As earning a minimum nominal return over a short—say, one-year—horizon makes no obvious contribution to the economics of the pension system, their value as tools in the management of defined benefit employer pension plans would appear to be limited.

6. There is no scientific survey behind the assertion that these contribution rates are "typical." However, they are in the middle of a sample of results from large, mainstream pension plans where the author has had personal involvement.

7. Sixty-forty equity-debt continues to be a good rule of thumb for where the median asset mix in a large sample of U.S. pension funds might come out. The ratio for Canadian funds is more like 50–50. A government rule that forces Canadian funds to invest 90 percent of their assets inside Canada—combined with a relatively high risk, low liquidity resources-biased stock market—is likely responsible for the weighting differential.

8. William Sharpe's *Investments,* Prentice-Hall, 1978, is a good place to start for those interested in pursuing the theoretical aspects of the risks and rewards of market timing. Robert H. Jeffrey's "The Folly of Stock Market Timing," *Harvard Business Review,* July–August 1984, presents a decidedly pessimistic view on the likely profitability of market timing-based strategies.

9. Figure 4–9 depicts a situation where a corporation has a main business and a pension business. In the preswap state, business assets are $10, there is no business debt, and hence balance sheet equity is $10. The pension plan has $5 of financial assets, $4 of accrued pension debt, and hence a $1 asset cushion.

   In the postswap state, corporation taxes payable are reduced by the net return of the equity portfolio after paying the interest on the bonds issued—less any taxes payable on the equity portfolio returns. The swap becomes a wash only if the tax rate on equity portfolio earnings equals the tax rate on regular business income.

   See Fisher Black and Moray Dewhurst's "A New Investment Strategy for Pension Funds," *Journal of Portfolio Management,* Summer 1981, for more on, as the article authors put it, "this irresistible plan to increase the corporation's value without increasing its risk."

10. Here's the "renaissance" consultant again. See note 6 in Chapter Three for an introduction to this consultant.

11. There are obviously actual scenario-related return and inflation numbers and an actuarial model of the pension system behind the sixth-year contribution rate projections. We acknowledge the importance of the specific projections and model here without providing the details of either. Specific projections and models are time-sensitive and adapted to unique situations. The focus of this book is on concepts and broad strategy.

12. Some readers might be taken aback by the real estate weight recommendation. We would suggest that generically there is little difference between equity positions in going-concern businesses that make widgets and ones that lease space to other businesses. There are differences, of course. One might be listed on a stock exchange; the other might be owned directly—possibly jointly with other pension funds.

   One might have debt on its balance sheet; the other one possibly not. These differences should not be of major consequence to a long-term investor with sufficient funds to diversify away the specific risk associated with individual equity investments—be they common stocks or ownership claims on real property.

FIGURE 4-9 The Equity-Bond Tax Arbitrage Swap

Pre-Swap Balance Sheets

Main

Business assets $10	Business debt 0
Financial assets Stocks 0 Bonds 0	Business equity $10

Pension

Financial assets Stocks $5 Bonds 0	Pension debt $4
	Asset cushion $1

Post-Swap Balance Sheets

Main

Business assets $10	Business debt $5
Financial assets Stocks $5 Bonds 0	Business equity $10

Pension

Financial assets Stocks 0 Bonds $5	Pension debt $4
	Asset cushion $1

Admittedly, stocks are easier to buy and sell. On the other hand, real estate has proved itself a better inflation hedge in recent decades. As to the relative sizes of stock and real estate markets, Ibbotson and Siegel (note 3, Chapter Three) report respective 1980 U.S. stock market and real estate market values (rounded) of $1,400 billion and $4,200 billion. Of the $4,200 billion, $490 billion was estimated to be in commercial nonresidential real estate, the area favored by pension funds. All these factors suggest to us that the consultant's 25 percent real estate recommendation is not unreasonable.

13. The smaller a national capital market, the more urgent it is to be able to invest outside of it if a balanced, efficient investment program is to be established. Investors in countries with small capital markets have not waited for portfolio theory to prove this to them.

    The Swiss and Dutch, for example, have lived by this credo for centuries. Significant benefits can be derived from international diversification even in larger capital markets such as the British, the German, the Japanese, and the Canadian. Even U.S. investors, with the world's largest capital market, can benefit from a degree of international diversification.

14. The "small cap" phenomenon—industry short form for the finding that listed small company stocks seem to systematically outperform listed large company stocks—is now well documented. Ground-zero venture capital investing with its hit-and-miss track record has also received a lot of attention in the media in recent years.

    There is also a less well explored—but large—area in between listed small firms and startup situations. Buyouts, spinoffs, second- and third-round venture financings all fit into this middle category. In the term *small business investments* all but the first of the above-mentioned areas are included. Listed smaller capitalization companies will be considered part of the fund's national stocks component.

CHAPTER FIVE

Investment Management: How Should the Investment Function Be Structured?

Investment management is a losers game.

—*C. Ellis*

Just as there are asset mix policy options, so there are policy options for investment management. Again, the policy range can be characterized as return-maximizing at one extreme and risk-minimizing at the other.

This chapter tackles the question of choosing an investment management philosophy and then structuring the investment function consistent with it. In doing so, the chapter also addresses the issues of capital market efficiency, of the value-added prospects of active management, and of the management of the investment function itself.

INVESTMENT MANAGEMENT STRUCTURE: THE ISSUES

Every business has a shorthand to convey its basic truths and beliefs. One of the favorites in the investment business is "asset mix is the most important investment decision." This basic investment tenet is certainly true—but only if it refers to asset mix policy as discussed in the previous chapter. In that context, it *is* the most important decision relating to the asset side of the pension system balance sheet. However, it is not always asset mix policy that the speaker has in mind.

The statement is often made in reference to the investment management activity we called "market timing" in the previous chapter. Recall this investment activity attempts to add value to the basic asset mix policy by shifting the mix away from the policy weights when markets—stock, bond, or cash—are expected to move up or down. Market timing, if practiced to an extreme, could significantly impact investment results but no more or less than security selection if it were practiced to the same extreme.[1]

In fact, neither market timing nor security selection activities are carried to extremes in practice. There is a good and simple reason for this. Nobody is sure enough of being right to "bet the ranch" on even the strongest-held views about the future.

So if views on markets or on individual securities are not clairvoyant enough to bet a lot, are they good enough to bet a little? How much is a little? What incremental return is it reasonable to associate with small bets? Bets relative to what benchmark? Are some investment managers more clairvoyant than others? Are some possibly good at one thing but not another?

The answers to these questions determine how much added value to look for from the investment management function. They also determine the structure the function must take on if the value-added expecta-

---

FIGURE 5-1 Investment Management Structure Options

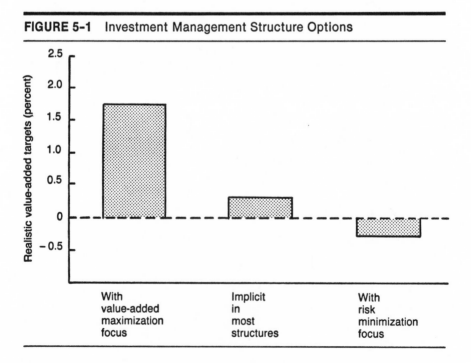

tion is to be realized. The options—as with asset mix policy—range from return-maximizing to risk-minimizing.

As with the asset mix policy options, the option range can be graphically depicted. Value-added in Figure 5-1 should be thought of as relative to a predetermined passive investment program that could be implemented instead of the value-added approach. Thus the zero percent baseline indicates what the passive policy would have achieved.

In the chapter sections that follow we examine these three approaches to asset mix policy implementation in turn.

Risk-Minimizing Investment Management

A second basic tenet in the investment business is that there is no free lunch in the capital markets. Reaching out for incremental return over what an asset mix policy—passively implemented—would produce involves taking incremental risks. There are two types of risks that must be incurred. First, extra return volatility must be endured with an active—that is, nonpassive—approach to investment management. However, this risk factor can be controlled and need not be a major worry.

Maybe more importantly, selection risk must be incurred. That is, even after incurring the extra return volatility, management fees, and transaction costs there is no guarantee that active management will, over the long haul, produce incremental pension fund return. Some investment managers will produce incremental return over the next few years—but which ones? Even the most exhaustive search for prospective (retrospective does not count) value-added managers does not guarantee their identification.

Given these realities, a decision not to incur the incremental risks and costs of active investment management can make good sense. One of the benefits of passively implementing an asset mix policy is focus. Only two things matter. Proper diversification within each asset class is important. Cost-effectiveness is equally important. Both attributes are unambiguous and subject to careful measurement. A plan sponsor can do worse than take a passive, low-cost route to asset mix policy implementation. Many do, in fact, do worse.[2]

The marginally negative value-added expectation depicted in Figure 5-1 for the risk-minimizing structure option reflects an important reality. Even a passive, cost-minimizing approach to implementing an asset mix policy costs money. Cash must be turned into security holdings. Portfolios require regular monitoring. Occasional rebalancings are required. Assets must be custodied and accounted for. All these activities imply fees payable. As a percentage of assets, though, these fees should not exceed one half of 1 percent for even small funds. They should be considerably lower for large funds.

Value-Added Investment Management: Where Are the Losers?

It takes only one, large, active investor with superior insight, superior information, or both to keep capital market prices "fair"—that is, fair in the sense that current prices and future prospects for each security in the market are properly aligned. Whenever this investor sees an under- or overvalued security, the investor will attempt to buy or sell it until it is fairly priced.

But who will trade against this superinvestor? Obviously only investors who are not aware of superinvestor's superior skill and superior sources of information. There is an important message in this. Consistent value-added management on the part of some managers requires a marketplace mirror image: it requires that value must be lost by others. A belief in the existence of winners requires an equal and opposite belief in the existence of losers.

If one is to develop a well-founded belief that value-added managers exist, maybe the best place to start is to attempt to identify who the value-losers might be. In this, we follow former *Financial Analysts Journal* editor Jack Treynor's brilliant exposition in the *Managing Investment Portfolios* text.[3]

First, there are the liquidity traders. These are people—either directly or through institutions—who simply want to put money into the market or take some out. These liquidity traders will transact with information traders if the latter happen to be offering the best price if the liquidity trader is buying or bidding the best price if the liquidity trader is selling. By always buying at the offer and selling at the bid, value is lost.

And then there are professional investors with information and its interpretation that is simply not as good as that of others. We believe the current structure and culture of the institutional investment management business—especially of the segment of the business that focuses on pension fund management—probably fosters a degree of systematic inferiority on the part of some information traders.

Why? Because, despite a steady stream of claims to the contrary, many investment management organizations still operate in a tradition-bound fashion. This tradition has its origin in investment managers being assigned the dual roles of risk controllers and value-added producers.

This duality began in the old insurance and personal trust investment environments and has carried over into the newer pension fund environment. Managers in this dual role position quite correctly make risk control the first priority and value-added production a secondary consideration. It is our observation that once a mindset has a primary risk control focus, systematically making money in the markets becomes very difficult.

Tradition-Bound Investment Management: How It Creates Opportunities for Others

Why is making money so difficult for risk controllers? There are a number of reasons. First, a blur develops between diversification-motivated decisions and money making-motivated decisions. The result is that many portfolio transactions end up being risk control rather than value-added production oriented. Potential for fuzzy thinking and implementation inconsistency results as a consequence.

Second, the risk control-oriented mindset needs to continuously demonstrate "prudence." While no longer required to be demonstrated legally at the individual security level,[4] this is still a perceived requirement. The result is a bias towards "quality" names in the portfolio. A quality investment in this context means a big, recognizable security issuer with steady earnings growth, brand name products or services, good liquidity for its securities, and so on.

A strong enough preference for the securities of issuers with these characteristics will lead to their return prospects being systematically reduced relative to "lower-quality" securities. This will happen despite the fact that most of the genuine investment risk associated with nonbrand name securities is diversifiable. Nonbrand name securities have, in fact, done extraordinarily well as a class.[5]

The need to demonstrate prudence often carries over into the organizational structure of the investment manager. Too many checks and balances stifle the creativity and boldness required to make money in the capital markets. These checks and balances can take the form of approved list rigidity where lengthy memoranda are required to get a name on the list (names often do not come off unless the issuer has gone bankrupt). They can also take the form of a hierarchical people-structure held together by titles, with everyone busy reporting to someone else.

A third exploitable dimension arises from—despite the underlying risk control orientation—a perceived requirement to appear aggressively value-added-oriented at quarterly client meetings. The result is a very short-term orientation to the money making-motivated decisions that are taken. Unfortunately, money making decisions with short horizons taken by risk control-oriented mindsets tend to produce group think phenomena in the capital markets.

The result is that much of the money chasing short-term performance ends up buying high and selling low. A corollary is that the longer-term horizon playing fields are uncrowded. Good slow ideas can suddenly become very profitable when the short termers eventually stumble across them. The slow idea expression is another Jack Treynor invention. It relates to investment ideas that have not yet gained widespread currency.[6]

A fourth opportunity arises out of the "game of inches" rather than the "long-ball" way that the majority of professional investors play the game. Costs are critically important in determining the winners and the losers in a game of inches. Yet cost control often gets nowhere near the attention it deserves. The result is a leakage of 1 percentage point per year or even more in transaction, custodial, and management costs in portfolios hard-pressed to gross half that back in value-added relative to passively managed portfolios.[7]

Finally, investing does not only take place via highly centralized and competitive stock, bond, and cash auction markets. But finding extraordinary real estate and small business investment opportunities in local markets requires special people with entrepreneurial mindsets.[8] Not many are comfortable working for investment organizations where risk control is the predominant investment consideration.

Value-Added Investment Management: Ingredients for Success

Successful value-added investment managers, while they might have very different ways of making money for their clients, probably have a number of characteristics in common. Table 5–1 lists six. Of the six, the first might well be the most important. No doubt, plan sponsors are often their own worst enemies in creating an environment conducive to money making investment management.

The first characteristic deserves further elaboration. Clients have played an important role in creating value-losing investment management environments. As we asserted above, leaving an investment manager to cope with both risk control and making money for the fund cre-

---

TABLE 5-1 Six Characteristics of Value-Added Management

---

1. Clients who will bear the responsiblity for risk control.
2. A focus on making money, not controlling risk.
3. A simple, unencumbered organizational structure.
4. Being contrarian rather than talking contrarian.
5. Reverence for controlling client costs.
6. Willing to look at unconventional ways of making money.

---

ates a no-win situation. It is no-win for both the client and the investment manager.

The lose-lose situation usually starts when the client's unrealistic performance expectations are acceded to by the manager. When they are not met, cognitive dissonance—a marvelous shortform for describing a relational state between two parties—begins to permeate client-manager meetings.

People say the things they think their role requires. They often do not say the things needed to clear the air to develop, for example, a mutual understanding of who is responsible for risk control—nor to develop, as a further example, a mutual understanding of the strengths and weaknesses of the investment organization as a value-added manager.

The result of this not atypical situation is predictable: loose risk control, value-losing investment management, and high manager turnover, which has its own built-in costs. How to break this vicious circle? By the client understanding that the pension fund is indeed the asset side of a financial subsidiary of the corporation.

Therefore, it is the corporation that is responsible for risk control. As we have seen, the main lever for exercising this responsibility is asset mix policy. Investment management structure and its staffing is a secondary—but not unimportant—lever.

The risk minimizing approach to investment management structure and staffing has already been examined and found both feasible and attractive in its focus and simplicity. For a return-maximizing approach to compete, it also must be endowed with focus and simplicity. This means there can be no ambiguity about why value-added managers are hired, where they fit in the total scheme of things, and what results are expected from them.

Table 5-2 itemizes the essence of the understanding that must be reached between client and value-added manager for a win-win situation to develop.

TABLE 5-2 Ingredients of a Win-Win Relationship

---

1. The client acknowledges responsibility for risk control.
2. A passive but implementable investment program that specifically (and therefore measurably) states how the money in question would be invested in the absence of value-added management is identified.
3. A long-term value-added target relative to this passive alternative is negotiated between the client and the manager. It should be an ambitious but achievable target. The logical consequence that, as a result, shorter-term performance will occasionally be poor should be explicitly acknowledged.
4. The basis-for-termination ground rules are established at the start. These rules should focus on such considerations as consistency of investment philosophy and the people implementing it. They should explicitly exclude short-term performance as a basis for termination.

Value-Added Management: How Much Extra Return?

Earlier in this chapter we suggested a 2 percent value-added target with an investment structure designed to maximize value-added in Figure 5-1. The time has come to justify this number.

In addition to the investment mandate given the manager by the client, there are three further considerations. How much value-added potential do capital markets provide? How much of the potential can be converted into realization? And, finally, how successful can you assume the process of finding superior value-added managers to be?

The potential for generating extraordinarily high rates of return in the capital markets is almost beyond comprehension. A volume of studies have shown the tremendous profit potential in correctly timing overall stock, bond, and cash market moves, in timing sector moves, in selecting the right securities within sectors, in selecting the right real properties, etc.[9] Excess return potential of 10 or even 20 or 30 percent is theoretically available each year.

How much of it can be converted into pension fund value-added? Very little of it. Why? Because capital markets—especially North American capital markets—generally do a good job of pricing investments today in line with their prospects for good news and bad news tomorrow. Even the most skillful value-added managers will not bat 1.000 in this type of capital market.

What can they realistically be expected to bat? Well, taking 0.500 to be random—and therefore having zero profit potential—they obviously have to bat over 0.500 (is this proof investing is a tougher game than baseball?). But how much over 0.500? There is evidence that it is very tough to get more than half way towards batting 1.000.[10]

The result is that only a small fraction—maybe somewhere between one tenth and one quarter—of capital market profit potential is capturable by even the most skillful managers. Translating the suggested 10 percent to 30 percent profit potential range into actuality can be done with some simple multiplication.

One tenth of 10 percent is 1 percent. One quarter of 30 percent is 7.5 percent. Deducting maybe 0.5 percent for management fees, the range becomes 0.5 to 7 percent. The distribution of value-added managers is probably not normal through this range. Likely, there are more managers at the lower end of the range than at the upper end.

Not only that, but it is likely that in the process of assembling a value-added management team, some managers with no superior skills will, despite best efforts to the contrary, end up on it.

The combination of these realities and judgments leads us to suggest that an overall fund value-added target of 2 percent is an outer limit target. And it is only achievable with an investment structure and associated mandates geared totally towards value-added maximization.

Actual Pension Fund Investment Management Structures: Their Implied Value-Added Targets

An examination of actual pension fund investment programs would confirm most are not geared to value-added maximization. Whether consciously done or not, large components of most pension funds are, in effect, passively managed.[11] If not submitted to value-added management, incremental fund return is unlikely to materialize.

The middle option in Figure 5–1 implies a fund investment structure where over half of the fund's assets are managed in passive or near passive modes. The remainder is subjected to value-added management. A much reduced, but possibly more realistic, overall net fund value-added target—in the 0.5 percent per annum range—results.

Recall that these targets are relative to the return that would be produced by an implementable risk-minimizing investment structure. Such a structure will produce the asset mix policy return less implementation costs—commissions, custodial and management fees—of maybe 0.25 percent per annum for a medium-sized pension fund. Adding 0.5 percent then means producing a net fund return 0.25 percent per annum above rather than below the pre-implementation cost asset mix policy return.

Earning a 0.5 percent per annum return increment over the long term would measurably impact the "profitability" of the pension subsidiary. We saw in the asset mix policy chapter such a return increment was equivalent to a 10 percent to 15 percent reduction in the cost of supporting the pension liabilities.

Having an investment management structure consistent with the achievement of 0.5 percent value-added does not guarantee its realization, of course. The only certainty with a structure geared to produce value-added is that it will cost more to operate than a risk-minimizing (passive) structure.

In fact, this incremental cost is probably in the 0.25 to 0.5 percent per annum area, depending on the size of the fund. Consequently, if no gross value-added is actually produced, the fund actually could be 0.25 to 0.5 percent per annum worse off than with the risk (and cost) minimizing investment structure.

With this background, let's return to the deliberations taking place at ALPHA Corporation. With the asset cushion and asset mix policy decisions behind it, ALPHA's management is ready to look at the question of how it wants the pension assets to be managed.

ALPHA'S PENSION FUND GOALS AND ASSET MIX POLICY DECISIONS: HOW WILL THEY IMPACT THE INVESTMENT STRUCTURE DECISION?

ALPHA's management has already given the structure question considerable thought, if only in broad terms. As part of its statement of pension fund goals, ALPHA's management had written:

- The fund's investment policy will be structured so that the anticipation of a 4½ percent long-term real rate of return is reasonable. This anticipation is based on an assumption of 2½ percent long-term national income growth in real terms. Asset mix policy is to add 1½ percent through the assumption of more equity risk than carried by the composite national market portfolio. The investment management program is to add an additional ½ percent through successful active management in a number of fund components.

In answer to the investment policy questionnaire question dealing with investment management, ALPHA's management had said:

Investment Management	**Do we believe active management can add value? Y/N** "Yes." **Do we believe we can identify active managers who will be successful—before rather than after the fact? Y/N** "We are by no means certain we can. However, we are willing to take some calculated risks here. The fund's exposure to active management will be carefully controlled and monitored."

The responses suggest ALPHA's management is not predisposed to try and hit the long ball with its pension fund investment program. However, it does intend to establish a value-added dimension in the program. A ½ percent value-added target has been set.

The decided-on asset mix policy provides the context in which this ½ percent is to be earned. It is shown in Figure 5–2. Management realized it was not realistic to set identical ½ percent value-added goals for all six fund components identified in the expanded version of the policy. Some fund components would appear to offer much more fertile ground for value-added management than others.

FIGURE 5-2 ALPHA Corporation's Asset Mix Policy

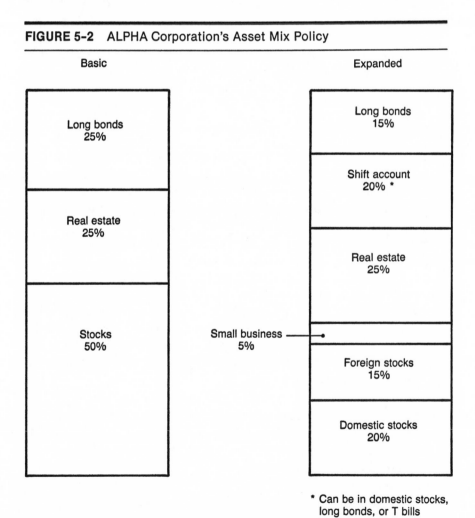

Basic

Expanded

Long bonds
25%

Real estate
25%

Stocks
50%

Long bonds
15%

Shift account
20% *

Real estate
25%

Small business
5%

Foreign stocks
15%

Domestic stocks
20%

* Can be in domestic stocks,
long bonds, or T bills

Also, some fund components have been assigned very specific roles through the formulation of asset mix policy. For example, the asset shift account (created as part of the asset mix policy for the fund—see Chapter Four) by its very nature will be an active, or value-added, fund component.

By contrast, the primary mission of the permanent long bond position is to act as a hedge against a deflationary environment in which the fund's equity investments would likely be doing very poorly. Given this role, it would seem inconsistent to permit a manager to move this component away from high-grade, long-duration debt instruments.

As they had done in the process of establishing both the asset cushion and asset mix policies, management decided to seek the advice of an outside consultant.[12] The mandate was to recommend an investment management structure consistent with already established pension fund goals and policies as well as management's stated views on value-added management.

The Consultant's Report: Investment Structure

The consultant came back with a plan that looked bolder, they assured ALPHA's management, than it actually was. It involved placing one third of fund assets in an explicit value-added management mode. It also involved a seemingly high number of investment management organizations. The consultant warned that, if the recommended structure was to be properly implemented, over 20 different firms might have to be hired to manage the $1.3 billion fund.

The recommended passive/active split within each of the six fund components is shown in Table 5-3. Under the active allocation column, the first number refers to the recommended number of managers to be employed within the category. For example, five managers managing $25 million each are recommended in the domestic stocks category. Note that the sum of the passive and value-added allocations adds up to the total fund value of $1.3 billion.

The first thing needing an explanation was the seemingly large number of managers being recommended. No, the consultant assured ALPHA's management, there was no intent to create new jobs for the consultant community! Indeed, as part of this current assignment the consultant intended to explain how ALPHA itself could staff the positions and monitor results without a great deal of consultant assistance.

The rationale for the large number lay, instead, in the nature of the

TABLE 5-3 Recommended Passive/Value-Added Split for Fund

	Passive Allocation ($ millions)	Active Allocation ($ millions)		
Permanent risk capital:				
Domestic stocks	$215	5 × $25	=	$125
Real estate	$245	4 × $20	=	$ 80
Small business	0	10 × $ 6.5	=	$ 65
Foreign securities	$145	2 × $25	=	$ 50
Permanent debt capital:				
Long bonds	$275		0	
Shift account				
Stocks/bonds/T-bills	0	2 × $50	=	$100
Totals	$880			$420
Percent of fund	68%			32%

mandates the consultant had in mind for the value-added managers. Each, in its own way, would receive a make money mandate. To impress on each manager the seriousness with which the mandate was to be taken, diversification inside each of manager portfolios would be purposely limited. Instead, the managers would be encouraged to invest to win, not to tie.

Diversification would still be achieved, but it would be achieved across manager portfolios, not within them. To further this intent, value-added managers would be selected keeping their approach to investing in mind. Care would have to be taken that, for example, not all five domestic stocks value-added managers were chartists or sector rotators or low P/E stock buyers—or that, as a further example, all four real estate value-added managers were West Coast shopping center specialists.

The consultant's recommended approach to investment structure was supported with analyses at the individual components level.

Domestic Stocks: A Recommended Approach

The point of departure here was the consultant's observation that most common stock portfolios at the individual manager level are traditionally highly diversified. This is easily defended in a situation where there is only one stock portfolio and where risk control is a consideration. This has traditionally, of course, been a typical situation.

The consultant argued, however, that there was a better way. If the typical portfolio was 90 percent passive and 10 percent active,[13] why pay active management fees on 100 percent of the portfolio? Why not formally index—that is, manage passively—90 percent of the portfolio at a much lower management fee and pay the higher active management fee on only the 10 percent beng managed that way?

But once one proceeds down that logic track, the previous questions prompt further questions. If it is worth paying the higher management fee on 10 percent of the portfolio, why stop there? What, for example, would the risk/reward characteristics be in the situation where there were 10 different active 10 percent pieces? Might these characteristics not be superior to the risk/reward characteristics of the original 90 percent passive–10 percent active blend?

The answer to the all-important last question is that, in all likelihood, the risk/reward characteristics of a portfolio where the money is equally allocated between 10 value-added managers would indeed be superior to those of the original 90 percent–10 percent blend. There are some caveats. The value-added managers must indeed be value-adding—not losing—managers. They must go about the business of making money in the stock market differently. If this is the case, the total stock portfolio will be considerably less risky than any of its 10 pieces.[14]

To help make these important points, the consultant sketched them out graphically. Figure 5–3 contrasts the risk/reward characteristics of the two possible starting points. One is the original single stock portfolio with its built in 90 percent passive–10 percent active blend. The other possibility is to start with 10 more aggressive subportfolios, each with a "make money" mandate.

Note that each of the subportfolios offers considerably more reward—in terms of expected value-added to a passive alternative—than the 90–10 blend. However, each piece also has considerably more uncertainty as to what its actual return will be. This is denoted by the width of the vertical bar above (good news) and below (bad news) the exptected value-added outcome. The expected outcome is denoted by the dot.

Figure 5–4 shows what happens when the subportfolios are combined into a single portfolio. The original single portfolio with the passive/value-added blend is also the final portfolio. Note that the 10 subportfolio option appears to violate the previously cited "no free lunch in the capital markets" principle. The 3 percent value-added expectation associated with each piece is maintained when the pieces are collectively seen as a single portfolio. However, the risk of the whole is smaller than the risk of each of the parts.[15]

FIGURE 5-3   Alternative Risk/Reward Trade-Offs: Step 1

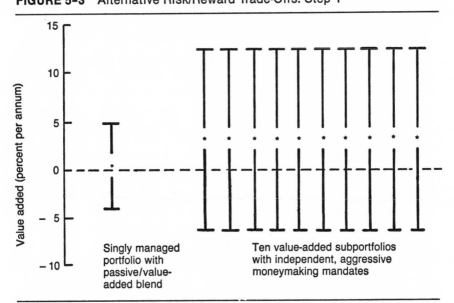

FIGURE 5-4   Alternative Risk/Reward Trade-Offs: Step 2

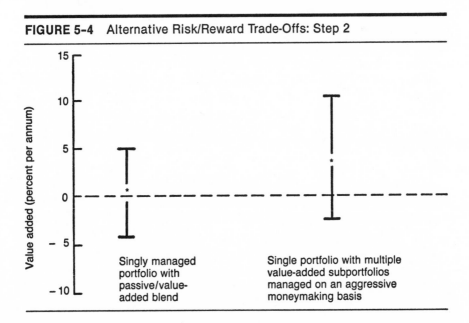

How can this situation exist in an almost efficient capital market? Well, partially through exploiting traditional thinking that automatically lumps passive and value-added management together in single packages. And partially by assumption. The assumptions are threefold.

First, sufficient successful value-added managers can be found to create the pieces. Second, these managers have different enough investment styles that the highly uncertain investment experience within each of the pieces is indeed more predictable at the aggregate portfolio level. Third, there are clients willing to give the managers true money making mandates.

There is still a further assumption. Widescale adoption of the recommended approach would eventually lead to its self-destruction. Spending the time and energy needed to get the approach operational implies a judgment that it will not be so widely adopted as to render it ineffective. The consultant expressed the view that the odds were heavily against a widescale, effective adoption of the recommended approach. It was too unconventional and too dependent on the successful selection of successful (tomorrow, not yesterday) money managers.

The consultant anticipated the obvious question that would be asked by ALPHA's very practical management team at this point. What evidence exists that this elegant design will actually work in practice? Fortunately, the consultant had recently had the opportunity to study two actual structures of this nature after they had been in operation for two years.[16]

Domestic Stocks: Experience with the Recommended Approach

To evaluate the actual experience of the two structures, benchmark experience is needed to provide a proper context. The benchmark suggestion of a 3 percent value-added expectation for a 10 percent value-added standard deviation has already been made (see note 15). These numbers related to each managed subportfolio and a one-year investment horizon.

To relate the actual experience to the 3 percent/10 percent benchmark, the benchmark needs to be converted to monthly equivalents. The monthly equivalent of 3 percent/10 percent is 0.3 percent/2.9 percent.[17] Table 5-4 provides the monthly risk/reward experience for two domestic stocks investment programs in operation for two years. Note that both structures have five subportfolios. There is zero overlap in the sense that there are no structure I managers in structure II, or vice versa.

TABLE 5-4 Two Domestic Stocks Investment Programs: Actual Experience with Highly Focused Investing over a Two-Year Period

	Structure I			Structure II	
	Average Monthly Value-Added	Value-Added Standard Deviation		Average Monthly Value-Added	Value-Added Standard Deviation
Manager A	−0.1%	2.9%	Manager F	0.5%	2.2%
Manager B	0.8%	3.0%	Manager G	0%	1.6%
Manager C	0.7%	3.0%	Manager H	0.3%	2.2%
Manager D	0.6%	3.4%	Manager I	0.6%	2.6%
Manager E	0.6%	2.5%	Manager J	−0.2%	1.9%
Averages	0.5%	3.0%		0.2%	2.1%
Portfolio	0.5%	2.4%	Portfolio	0.2%	1.3%

The consultant made a number of observations on the two-year results. First, both structures were successful in delivering positive value-added over the observation period. Relative to the 0.3 percent per month benchmark, structure I overperformed; structure II underperformed. Note that the portfolio result equaled the average of the results of the five subportfolios. This is a direct result of regularly rebalancing the weights of the five pieces towards equality.[18]

Second, there was a distinct difference in the degree of aggressiveness with which the structure I and structure II subportfolios were being managed. The structure I pieces had value-added return standard deviations averaging 3.0 percent—equal to the suggested benchmark. Structure II pieces were managed considerably more conservatively, with the average standard deviation almost one-third lower at 2.1 percent.

Third, structure I pieces did not diversify as well against each other as structure II pieces. At 2.4 percent, structure I's portfolio standard deviation is only 20 percent lower than the average of the five pieces. By contrast, structure II's portfolio standard deviation, at 1.3 percent, is almost 40 percent lower.[19]

The consultant concluded that, while structure I had produced more value-added over the observation period, structure II was less likely to produce unpleasant surprises. Both structures could be improved. Structure I needs more manager diversification. Structure II needs to encourage its managers to be more aggressive in pursuing value-added.

In providing ALPHA with these results, the consultant wanted to make an important point. With an appropriate monitoring system, the kind of midcourse corrections suggested for structures I and II can be implemented. There is no need to "fly blind" once structures of the recommended type are put in place.

In recommending ALPHA commence with a $125 million five subportfolio program, the consultant did not mean to suggest that that was the total capacity of operating a focused domestic stock investment program. It could eventually be larger. However, the recommended scale attempted to balance the minimum required to achieve diversification and fee economies with the maximum initial commitment ALPHA might be willing to make to this area.

With the consultant's approach to constructing value-added investment programs established in considerable detail as it relates to domestic stocks, the other component commentaries were briefer.

Foreign Securities

The international investment management scene does not lend itself as easily to the many focused subportfolios approach to value-added management just described for domestic stocks. The reason for this, the consultant suggested, was practical—not theoretical. The search time required to find investment specialists within each of 5 or even 10 or more foreign capital markets would be daunting. Further, there is no guarantee that such a search would be successful, especially in the smaller markets. Extensive disaggregation of the foreign component would also be very expensive with both per dollar management and custodial fees considerably higher, especially for smaller amounts.

However, these factors do not totally prevent the establishment of a value-added investment program with characteristics like those described for the national stocks program. What it does mean is some urgency in finding more than one piece of the program from the same vendor. For example, a single firm might be hired to provide both market timing across all major national markets and currencies and security selection within these markets. Other firms, depending on their skills, might be asked to concentrate strictly on European or on the Pacific Rim capital markets.

The consultant suggested that almost two thirds of the money designated for foreign markets might have to be managed passively. This reflects an assessment that focused value-added investment management mandates are not yet understood by many of the firms that specialize in international investments. Rather than risk that the money end up in value-losing hands, better to have it managed in an explicitly passive, cost-minimizing fashion.

Real Estate and Small Business

The suggestion that only one third of the designated real estate money be put out with value-added mandates again reflects a practical judgment by the consultant. There simply is not a very large pool of value-added real estate managers out there equipped to deal with pension funds on pension funds' terms. While no real estate money has been as formally "indexed" as stock money has, good practical proxies for it exist. They are the large open-end pooled real estate funds operated by financial institutions with long histories of investing their own moneys in real estate.[20]

The keys to successful investment programs in the small business area are, of course, both diversification and specialization. With the norm that out of 10 investments, 2 die, 2 become "living dead," 4 return no more than what perfectly safe investments do, it leaves it up to 2 super winners to carry the day. That is the diversification key.

However, the 2–2–4–2 batting average is not automatic. It requires the study of possibly hundreds of proposals to find the 10 investments actually worthy of funding. It takes special talent to reduce the hundreds to the 10 with a legitimate chance to produce a big payoff. That is the specialization key.

The Asset Mix Shift Account

The asset mix shift account was created as part of the establishment of an asset mix policy for ALPHA Corporation. ALPHA's management was not comfortable without some means to change the fund's actual asset mix over the shorter term. However, the consultant reminded them that anticipating shorter-term movements in stock prices and interest rates and moving actual dollars based on these anticipations takes special skills. Indeed, it is as much a specialty as venture capital investing and hence automatically a value-added fund component.

The other thing the consultant could now make clearer is the need to have a winning rather than losing approach to setting up the market timing component. As with domestic stocks, adding value means offense, not defense. Here, offense might well involve being 100 percent in T-bills for 3, 6, or even 12 months. It also involves a willingness to pick up the telephone one day and move the entire component out of T-bills into stocks or long bonds. If such moves are to be successful, they will generally be made while the crowd is still heading the other way.

This approach, the consultant reminded ALPHA management, does not mean risk control has been abandoned. It does mean that it is in the hands of the pension plan sponsor, not the investment manager.

How does the sponsor control risk? In two complementary ways: first, by establishing an overall policy asset mix, and second, by deciding what percentage of the total fund is to be subjected to active market timing.

In ALPHA's case there is already a decision in principle to make its pension fund's market timing component 20 percent of the total fund, or $260 million. This 20 percent could all be in T-bills, or all in long bonds, or all in domestic stocks. If it was all in bonds, the overall fund bond position would rise from its minimum 15 percent to its maximum 35 percent. If it was all in domestic stocks, the overall fund domestic stock position would rise from its minimum 20 percent to its maximum 40 percent.

Recall that in Table 5–3 the consultant recommended the money be spread across two market timers. This would create a third level of risk control if managers with differing approaches to market timing could be found. The reasoning here is completely analogous to that presented for domestic stocks. The reason for starting the two managers off with $50 million each was again based on a judgment that ALPHA might want to ease into this approach to asset mix shifting.

Long Bonds

Asset mix policy carved out a special role for long bonds. Their primary role is damage control for the fund should an extended period of deflation occur. Out of the original 25 percent position, 4 percentage points would be moved to the asset mix shift account. With these considerations in mind, the consultant recommended a good portion of the remaining 21 percent be placed in stripped coupons or principal repayments of government bonds. Ideally, all strips would be 20 years or longer in length and of AAA quality.

The consultant recommended that this permanent long bond component not be subjected to any form of value-added management. This would ensure that there would be no ambiguity with respect to its role. Also, the value-added potential within a bond position constrained to be both long and very high grade is very limited.

The consultant did want to make one further point about bonds as a pension fund investment. Historically, low-grade bonds have, on average, earned excess returns in line with those promised via higher yields than have high-grade bonds at time of purchase.[21] For long-term investors with enough money to build diversified portfolios of low-grade bonds, these large risk premiums represent a special opportunity to make money.

However, the consultant suggested that this opportunity be exploited through the equity rather than the debt part of the pension fund. Possibly, one of the specialists inside the domestic stocks and real estate value-added components could focus on making money out of securities that looked like debt but in fact represented equity-type positions.

Managing the Investment Structure

The consultant had stressed the importance of managing the pension system as a financial subsidiary of ALPHA throughout the assignments undertaken for ALPHA so far. The time had come once again to put the analogy to use. While there is little to do in the way of liability management in pension systems—these are determined as part of overall corporate compensation policy—there is a great deal to do in the way of asset management.

Asset management in the context used by the consultant means implementing senior management (probably with board approval) policy decisions regarding the asset side of the pension subsidiary. Thus, it takes asset cushion policy as a given. It also takes senior management's attitudes and views on the opportunities and risks that defined benefit pension plans present to an employer as givens. But within these givens, the pension asset management function offers great scope for value-added in its own right.

While senior management decides on asset mix policy, it is the asset management function that shapes the choices. While it is senior management that decides on the kind of asset management function it wants, its effective operation only starts once someone has been given bottom-line responsibility for its operation. Part of that operation is shaping its organizational design, staffing the positions in it, and meeting established value-added targets within the decided-on asset mix policy.

An early decision that must be taken in designing the asset management organization is the internal/external investment management split. While at first blush it would seem neat and tidy to have all investment functions carried out by outside investment agents, it should not be a foregone conclusion. There is considerable value, the consultant argued, in having an in-house nucleus of investment people. This becomes increasingly true the larger the fund.

First, an in-house management dimension could reduce the cost of managing ALPHA's pension assets. The recommended permanent long bond position is a good case in point. An external management fee as low as 0.2 percent would still amount to over $500 thousand per annum. Using this $500 thousand internally would go some way to funding an internal staffing budget! There is no reason to believe this type of bond fund could not be competently managed by a small ALPHA pension investment staff.

Second, it helps to have some people steeped in the investment culture on the inside. Even if most if not all of the value-added managers to be employed are outside managers, understanding how they make money—or at least how they are supposed to make money—is important. It was the consultant's observation that this understanding is very difficult to acquire by simply reading books on money management and taking guided tours through investment manager offices. There simply is no substitute for practical experience.

ALPHA's Decisions

Management astutely realized that the consultant had placed two policy decisions in front of them from which specific operational decisions would flow. First, would they adopt the internal/external, passive/value-added structure philosophy being proposed? Second, were they prepared to put a single individual in charge of pension asset management?

They admitted to being intrigued by thinking in terms of a four-dimensional investment management structure for the pension fund. Each dimension appeared to potentially have something to contribute to the effective management of ALPHA's pension assets. Conversely, there was nothing in their beliefs or corporate culture that would automatically exclude any of the four dimensions.

Management was also favorably disposed to the idea of placing a single individual in a position of defined responsibility, with his or her outputs clearly measurable. ALPHA has vice presidents with bottom-line responsibility for all its other operating divisions. Some of these divisions do not approach the pension fund in its potential impact on the corporate balance sheet and income statement. So why not a Vice President, pension asset management?

In their usual decisive fashion, they made affirmative decisions on both issues. Table 5–5 shows how they summarized their decisions in a presentation to the board pension committee.

Having created a position with the listed key responsibilities, ALPHA's management realized it made no sense for them to judge the merits of the many specific consultant structure recommendations. If a Vice-President, pension asset management is given the responsibility to implement asset mix policy and to produce an increment of value-added, this individual also has to have the authority to make it happen. Part of that authority involved staffing the investment function.

TABLE 5-5   Management Decisions Relating to ALPHA'S Pension Fund Investment Structure

---

Decision 1: Adoption of the four-dimensional structure as shown below with dollar allocations into each of the four quadrants to be decided.

	Passive Management	Value-Added Management
Internal Management		
External Management		

Decision 2: Creation of a new senior management position titled Vice President, pension asset management. Key responsibilities are listed below.

- Asset mix policy recommendations to senior management at least once a year.
- Asset mix policy implementation below a negotiated cost ceiling. Ceiling level to be negotiated between the Vice President, pension asset management and senior management.
- The production of an increment of pension fund return over what a purely passively implemented policy asset mix would have delivered. Size of increment to be negotiated between the Vice President, pension asset management and senior management.

In so doing, the quadrants of the investment structure matrix (see Table 5–5) would automatically be filled in. Thus the monies to be allocated to internal and external investment agents would be indicated as well as the split between moneys to be managed in passive and value-added management modes.

It was with considerable satisfaction that ALPHA's senior management team observed that this latest round of decisions marked an important occurrence. With the asset cushion and asset mix decisions already made, only the policy decisions related to the actual management of the pension assets remained. Now they too have been made.

The new approach to the financial management of ALPHA's pension system is ready to go operational!

CHAPTER NOTES

1. Impact on portfolio performance is determined by two things: impact potential and degree to which it can be realized. Taking, for example, one-year holding periods, 20 percent is typically used as the holding period return standard deviation for the stock market as a whole. Obviously, significant value can be added to (or lost from) a buy and hold strategy by boldly and correctly (incorrectly) timing market moves. This is often presented as evidence that the asset mix—meaning market timing—is more important than stock selection.

    What is overlooked when such an assertion is made is the size of the one-year holding period standard deviation of the nonmarket component of a typical stock. It is maybe 30 percent compared to the market's 20 percent. The conclusion is that, practiced to an extreme, stock selection is more important than market timing. Market timing only becomes more important if it is practiced a lot while selection is only practiced a little.

2. It is widely known that for long holding periods the median fund in large samples of broadly comparable managed funds tends to underperform a fair benchmark passive portfolio. Often, the degree of benchmark underperformance for the median fund approximates the sum of transaction costs and management fees for the fund.

3. The reference is to Chapter Twelve titled *Implementation of Strategy: Execution,* by Jack L. Treynor in *Managing Investment Portfolios,* edited by John L. Maginn and Donald L. Tuttle, published by Warren, Gorham, & Lamont, 1983. In our own reference to creative, value- adding, and tradition-bound investment firms, it would be a mistake to attempt to categorize them by size, geography, or type of investment institution. Instead, we would prefer to categorize them by the presence or absence of the six characteristics of Table 5–1.

4. ERISA in the United States, for example, explicitly defines prudence as a portfolio rather than individual security concept. Canadian authorities are on record as favoring a move in this direction.

5. The nonbrand name phenomenon is probably the major reason behind the now widely studied "small cap" effect. It appears that small capitalization stocks have systematically outperformed large capitalization stocks both in the United States and Canadian stock markets for decades now. To a lesser degree, stocks with low earnings multiples have systematically outperformed stocks with higher earnings multiples. This might well be another manifestation of the nonbrand name phenomenon.

6. Jack Treynor's associates Bob Boldt and Hal Arbit elaborate in "Efficient Markets and the Professional Investor," *Financial Analysts Journal,* July–August 1984.

7. Batterymarch Financial Management President Dean LeBaron wrote about this in detail in "Reflections on Market Inefficiency," *Financial Analysts Journal,* May–June 1983.

8. It is our observation that value-added direct investing requires individuals—often working in small two- or three-person partnerships—who spend little time in the of-

fice. Instead, they are out on a neverending search for deals. The fact that through their fee formula they usually get a participation any deal they do for a pension fund—or a group of funds via a closed-end fund—is viewed negatively by some plan sponsors. Such plan sponsors do not understand the culture of the direct investment professional and probably should not get involved with them.

9. Again, the source of all this reward potential is no mystery. Even small changes in long-term cash flow prospects in long duration investments—stocks, real property, long bonds—will lead to large changes in their capital values in the short term. Such prospects changes occur all the time. Some are related to macro factors—potentially affecting the prospects for whole classes of securities. Others are purely micro in the sense that they relate to only one issuer.

10. This author spent a good deal of time researching this predictive accuracy issue during the 1970s. The results of it are probably best summarized in "Can Active Management Add Value?" by Keith Ambachtsheer and James Farrell Jr., *Financial Analysts Journal,* November–December 1979.

11. While billions of pension fund dollars are now formally passively managed, a good deal more gets this treatment indirectly by being placed with managers who—within the confines of one fund—manage actively at the edges while holding most of the money in a passive core.

12. ALPHA's management has been very astute in their selection of consultants. They have correctly looked for people who are not only knowledgeable and creative, but who can focus on ALPHA's needs without having to meet any needs of their own other than collecting a fair fee for services performed. This becomes the more difficult the more the consulting organization uses consulting assignments to sell ongoing services of an actuarial, performance measurement, or money management nature.

13. R squareds of 90 percent are not atypical when monthly stock portfolio returns are regressed against a broad market index. The implication is that the remaining 10 percent of the portfolio's return variability is related to other than broad market considerations. Instead, it is related to the ways in which a particular portfolio differed from the broad market portfolio over the observation period.

14. For example, if each of the 10 pieces had nonmarket risk in it equivalent to a one-year return standard deviation of 10 percent, a portfolio comprising the 10 pieces—equally weighted—would have a considerably lower one-year standard deviation. If the 10 nonmarket risks were perfectly independent, the overall portfolio's nonmarket risk would only be about 3 percent.

If, as is more likely, there is some positive correlation between some of the nonmarket returns of some of the pieces, the risk reduction might be from the original 10 percent to maybe 5 or 6 percent. Interestingly, this about the level of nonmarket risk for the typical 90 percent passive–10 percent active blend singly managed portfolio.

This discussion is the portfolio theory equivalent of what some consultants now call the "style offset" approach to selecting a team of money managers. Technically, it means finding managers with different enough ways of going about the business of making money that their nonmarket returns are independent.

15. As suggested is normal in note 14 above, the nonmarket risks of the singly managed portfolio and the portfolio made up of the 10 separate pieces are about the same. These risks are represented graphically in both Figures 5-3 and 5-4 by the vertical lines centered by the dot representing the value-added expectation. The heighth—from bottom to top in each case—represents the expectation plus or minus, standard deviation.

This means there is an approximately 70 percent chance the actual return outcomes for one-year investment periods will fall within the range depicted by the bars. However, recall our previous caveat about the value-added expectations. While they are reasonable for successful value-added managers, there is no guarantee the actual managers selected will be value-added managers. In other words, the bars do not encompass manager selection risk.

16. Actually, it was this author who had the opportunity to study the two structures. Because they were part of a private study, the actual structures can not be identified. The numbers shown in Table 5–4 have been changed marginally from the original numbers. However, the original numbers led to conclusions identical to those based on the adjusted numbers reached by ALPHA's consultant.

17. Of course, 0.3 percent per month annualized produces more than 3 percent per year of value-added. However, if the 0.3 percent per month is before management fee, then 3 percent per annum could be earned after paying the fee. The 2.9 percent standard deviation was derived by applying the "square root rule," which in this case means dividing the original one-year 10 percent standard deviation by the square root of 12 in order to "monthize" it.

It is necessary to go through these procedures if the type of analysis discussed is to be performed. A key assumption is needed to make valid statements about one-year holding periods from an analysis based on one month holding periods. It must be reasonable to assume that the monthly portfolio return differences from those on a broad market index are serially uncorrelated. Fortunately, this tends to be a reasonable assumption for most portfolios most of the time.

18. Note that this rebalancing towards equality produces a practice opposite to that actually practiced by many plan sponsors. The implication of rebalancing towards equality is that the relatively worst performing sub-portfolios get the relatively most amount of new money. The relatively best performing sub-portfolios get the least. In practice, many plan sponsors do it the other way around.

19. If the monthly value-added components of the five sub-portfolios had been serially uncorrelated, the portfolio standard deviation for the structure I portfolio would have been 1.3 percent instead of the actual 2.4 percent. Consequently, the presence of significant positive correlation between the return components is indicated. This was confirmed by a direct test. The average correlation in structure I was 0.5. The equivalent numbers for structure II were 0.9 percent instead of the actual 1.3 percent. The implication of some positive correlation was confirmed by direct test. The average correlation in structure II was 0.1.

20. We are mainly speaking of life insurance companies here. The suggestion is that by allocating a pension fund's real estate money across a number of the large real estate pools, a highly representative market real estate portfolio would result. An alternative is to establish an in-house real estate investment function that concentrates on creating a well-diversified real estate component for the pension fund. A number of the large Canadian funds have successfully gone this route. Indeed, eight have gone beyond that and now own Morguard Limited, which has evolved into a major player in the Canadian (and more recently the U.S.) mortgage and real estate scene.

21. These findings were first documented in the landmark Braddock Hickman study *Corporate Bond Quality and Investor Experience, 1900 to 1943,* National Bureau Of Economic Research, 1958. Hickman showed that even during the Depression the risk premiums on lower-grade bonds more than compensated for the higher loss rate experience.

PART THREE

Business Operations

CHAPTER SIX

Policy Implementation: From Principles to Practices

Saying is one thing, doing is another.

—*Old French Proverb*

Making the business policy decisions is not enough. They must also be implemented. This chapter lists all the responsibilities that must be assigned. It also lists all the players to whom they could be assigned. The responsibilities and the players are brought together through a responsibility allocation matrix. This chapter also includes effectiveness descriptions for money managers.

To further the practicality of the ideas presented here, the chapter describes how ALPHA Corporation's Vice President, pension asset management actually puts such ideas into practice.

FROM SAYING TO DOING

The preceding chapters identified the policy issues surrounding the financial management of employer pension systems. For each of these issues, possible ways of thinking about them and dealing with them were discussed. Because the issues are pension fund goals and policies on asset cushion size, asset mix, and investment management structure, their resolution must take place at the highest levels. Consequently, we made regular reference throughout our discussions to "senior management" and "the board of directors."

All this is well and good. But unless policy decisions are converted into the work needed to actually get them implemented, all is for nought. This obvious connection has not been universally made by pension plan sponsors. It is still common to find a plan sponsor that treats its pension assets, sometimes well over $100 million, as a corporate nuisance. While all the appropriate policies might exist on paper, no one has bothered to ensure their effective implementation! Given the potential impact these assets have on the sponsor's financial health, this kind of neglect is difficult to fathom.

Thus we applaud ALPHA Corporation's top level decision makers for taking the actual implementation of its pension fund policy decisions very seriously. We also applaud their ability to differentiate between matters of corporate policy and matters of pension asset management operation. Quite correctly, we believe, they have decided to operate the pension investment function analogous to that of other corporate "businesses." Someone is put in charge, with the "output" of the business subject to measurable goals negotiated between the business manager and senior management.

What must not be lost sight of in this process of normalizing the pension asset management of function is that there are ways in which the pension business differs from other divisions. The assets of the business, while their good or poor performance impacts the fortunes of the sponsor in the same way that regular corporate assets do, are not corporate assets. One observer suggests that they are more like rented assets.[1] The use of these rented assets is subject to government regulation.

Also, while pension asset management must take the liabilty side of the pension balance sheet as a given, it is not a given at the corporate policy level. Benefit policy is an important dimension of overall compensation policy. The implementation of pension benefit policy has its own challenges. In financial terms, it involves servicing pension debt. In human terms, it means carrying through on a corporate promise to pay part of an employee's compensation after she or he is no longer on the active payroll. It is both a legal and a moral obligation employers must take very seriously.

SORTING OUT RESPONSIBILITIES

Sorting out responsibilities is a good place to start the policy implementation process. In its most condensed form, a particular pension system-related responsibility must be assigned to one of three organizational players: the board of directors, corporate management, or an appointed outside agent. These responsibilities will fall into one of three categories: policy-related, operations-related, or control-related. Further, they will have either an asset or liability (benefits) orientation.

TABLE 6-1 Responsibility Allocation Matrix: Overall System

	Board	Management	Outside Agents
Policy 1. Benefits 2. Asset cushion 3. Asset mix 4. Investment structure	Who is		
Operations 5. Staffing 6. Investment management 7. Asset custody and accounting 8. Benefit administration 9. Employee communications		Responsible	
Control 10. Asset/liability valuation, compliance, trusteeship 11. Investment management evaluation 12. Policies review			For what

Table 6-1 shows how the players and the pension system responsibilities to be allocated can be made to come together. This matrix is an excellent means of ensuring that all responsibilities are assigned—but assigned only once.

The importance of actually going through the matrix and sorting things out cannot be overestimated. It is critically important to get it straight between management and the board of directors where policy-making and approval starts and stops. This is true for both the asset and benefits side of the plan. It is equally important to do this responsibility alignment between management and outside agents, such as investment managers and actuaries.

A more refined matrix is required to get at the alignment of asset management responsibilities per se. In putting together this more detailed matrix, we take certain things as givens. We assume that the senior management team makes policy on both the asset and liability sides of the balance sheet, with a board of directors committee possibly playing an advise and consent role.

Table 6-2 distinguishes between this senior management team and a pension asset management team. Responsibility allocation between them and between outside agents and them is now at issue. This more

TABLE 6-2 Responsibility Allocation Matrix: Pension Assets

	Senior Management	Pension Asset Management	Outside Agents
Policy 1. Asset cushion 2. Asset mix 3. Investment structure 4. Fund value-added target 5. Budget	Who is		
Operations 6. Component value-added targets 7. Staffing—internal 8. Staffing—external 9. Component investment management—internal 10. Component investment management—external 11. Asset custody and accounting		Responsible	
Control 12. Asset/liability valuation, compliance, trusteeship 13. Component investment management evaluation 14. Fund and component value-added target review 15. Asset cushion policy review 16. Asset mix policy review			For what?

detailed matrix is consistent with the overall system matrix (Table 6-1). Indeed, there is ideally only one very large matrix that would ensure there were neither overlaps nor underlaps in the organization.

This matrix forces senior management—management responsible for the pension asset management function—and the outside agents—investment managers, consultants, performance measurers, etc.—to sort themselves out. A fully completed matrix would have one (and only one!) "R"—responsible for—per function listed. Each function might also have one or more "C"—to be consulted; or "W"—to do work.

There is another tool that can be very useful as a communication device when pension asset management responsibilities are in the process of being delegated. If job descriptions serve a useful purpose, it should be no less true for asset management than for any other field.

The job effectiveness description can communicate—in writing—vital information to candidates for investment management positions. This is true whether the candidate is an individual or an investment firm. In either case, it can also serve as a formal agreement between the sponsor and the manager. Table 6–3 shows what such a job effectiveness description should cover.

TABLE 6–3 An Investment Manager Job Effectiveness Description

---

Plan Sponsor:

Investment Manager:

Effective Contract Date:

Fund Investment Component to Be Managed:	As defined in the fund asset mix policy and/or description of the fund investment management structure.
Role of Component in Overall Fund Asset Mix Policy:	As described in the fund asset mix policy and/or description of the fund investment management structure.
Manager Mandate:	Describes any limitations that might be imposed in achieving performance standard(s).
Performance Benchmark:	States benchmark(s) against which actual results will be evaluated.
Performance Standards:	Sets expectation of actual component performance relative to benchmark.
Performance Tolerances:	Sets tolerance for possible underperformance of benchmark in relation to length of evaluation period.
Philosophy/Style:	The sponsor's understanding of the type of manager being hired.
Personnel	The sponsor's understanding as to who the key people in the investment firm are and how they will contribute to the performance of the sponsor's fund.
Reporting Requirements:	Sets out sponsor information requirements by type and frequency.
Termination:	States possible reasons for dismissal.
Fees:	Sets out remuneration, including method of calculation.
Brokerage Allocation:	Sets out sponsor expectations regarding investment manager's negotiation and disposition of brokerage commissions.
Agreement Signed By:	Both sponsor and manager sign agreement.

In the previous chapter we stressed the importance of making things perfectly clear, especially if a pension investment program is to have value-added components. The job description investment agreement provides a practical means of doing so.

Let us see how ALPHA Corporation uses the responsibility matrix and job description devices to go from saying to doing.

Responsibility Allocation at ALPHA Corporation

ALPHA's management came out of their deliberations on the investment management structure question with two priorities. First, it was imperative to fill the position of Vice President, pension asset management quickly. Second, decisions would have to be made on a number of organizational matters related to the pension system.

They identified a number of important attributes for someone to be successful in the VP-pension asset management position. The person had to be intellectually capable of understanding the relationship between the pension fund and the beneficiaries, the shareholders, and the regulators. This understanding should parallel that of ALPHA's senior management team. The person should be able and willing to use the authority that would go with the position to meet specific time-bound goals. These goals would be negotiated between the manager and top management.

The person should also have a knowledgeable and realistic perspective on the capital markets, in general, and on the investment management function, in particular. By this, management meant they wanted someone who, likely through some combination of experience and intuition, understood the "almost efficient" nature of the capital markets and its consequences for pension asset management.

As the search for this person commenced, management realized they would do well to sharpen the lines of authority between the board of directors and top management on pension-related issues. They had been struck during their deliberations on pension fund goals and asset cushion and asset mix policies that certain issues need a joint asset/liability focus to be addressed effectively. Historically, they acknowledged, they had let the benefits people worry about benefits and the financial people worry about the pension fund.

To get a more balanced perspective on pension policy issues, they would henceforth be handled by the management pension committee. The membership of this committee—the president; the senior vice president, finance; and the senior vice president, human resources—

gave ample testimony to the importance management would henceforth attach to resolving pension-related policy issues.

Management had also been struck by the ambiguity that surrounds some pension-related policy issues. The company's moral (but not legal) obligation to adjust pensions in pay for inflation is a case in point. Setting the lower and upper limits on the size of the pension asset cushion and the long-term gain/short-term pain trade-off in the asset mix policy decision are others.

It is exactly with these types of issues that a good board of directors can be helpful. While legally representing only the shareholders' interests, their experience and maturity should lead them to see those interests in the broadest terms. Such broad terms should encompass the nature of the obligations of the employer to inactive pension plan members and the relationship between corporate financial resources and the pension trust fund.

To tap the board's wisdom on these and related issues management invited the board to strike a board pension committee. Its role would be advisory, with the management pension committee being obliged to consult the board committee before making any final decisions on matters of pension policy.

The Vice President, Pension Asset Management Search

Finding the manager for the pension asset management "business" was clearly a management pension committee responsibility. They decided to use the responsibility allocation matrix: pension assets (see Table 6-4) as a communication, discussion, and candidate evaluation device. Their hope was that the matrix would help identify the right candidate and define the specifics of the position and its relationship to the management pension committee all at the same time.

After a number of near misses, ALPHA got the person they wanted. Here is how the management pension committee and the new VP-pension asset management decided to split up the responsibilities listed in the matrix. Recall that "R" means responsible for; "C", to be consulted; and "W", to do work.

Most of the responsibility assignments were predictable. Some, however, were the result of considerable discussion and sometimes lively debate. For example, the new VP-pension asset management argued that setting component value-added targets went with the asset management position. The overall fund target was simply the weighted average of the component targets and hence setting it was the responsibility of

TABLE 6-4 Responsibility Allocation Matrix: Pension Assets

	Senior Management	Pension Asset Management	Outside Agents
Policy			
1. Asset cushion	R	C	W
2. Asset mix	R	C/W	
3. Investment structure	R	C/W	
4. Fund value-added target	C	R	W
5. Budget	C	R	
Operations			
6. Component value-added targets		R	C/W
7. Staffing—internal	C	R	
8. Staffing—external	C	R	W
9. Component investment management—internal		R/W	
10. Component investment management—external			R/W
11. Asset custody and accounting			R/W
Control			
12. Asset/liability valuation, compliance, trusteeship	R	W	W
13. Component investment management evaluation		R	W
14. Fund and component value-added target review	C	R	
15. Asset cushion policy review	R	C	W
16. Asset mix policy review	R	C/W	
17. Investment structure review	R	C/W	

that position as well. The management pension committee granted the point, subject to being given the opportunity to understand how the value-added targets were arrived at.

The VP-pension asset management also insisted on having the responsibility for and authority to hire and terminate both internal and external investment professionals or firms. This followed logically from having the responsibility to meet fund value-added targets. Note the distinction between having the responsibility for staffing and the responsibility for actually managing a fund component. The latter responsibility may well be delegated to an outside agent.

Decisions concerning control-related responsibilities flowed from the same logic. The management pension committee formally recognized its fiduciary repsonsibilities for the fund under item 11—asset/liability valuation, compliance, trusteeship. Also, the management committee would exercise ultimate control of the asset management function under item 17—investment structure review.

But the pension asset manager was given the authority to make whatever operational changes were deemed appropriate to meet the value-added and cost targets. Hence, the manager had the responsibility for investment management and value-added evaluation and, if needed, revision.

Transforming the Asset Management Function

As part of the startup phase, the VP-pension asset management carefully studied the consultant report on investment structure. Given the extensive discussions that had already taken place between the VP and the management pension committee on this topic, the report contained no surprises. The major philosophical question was how successful the explicit passive/focused value-added split approach would be. The major practical question was the rate at which the approach could be implemented.

Table 5-3, which summarized these recommendations, is reproduced as Table 6-5 on the following page. In studying them, it was apparent to the new VP that a lot of good calls on investment talent would be required to make the value-added dimension of the investment program work. But it was comforting that the success of the total program was not dependent on any one such call.

There was, of course, a further reality. The $1.3 billion was currently being managed by three traditional managers, each with a 60 percent to 40 percent stock-bond guideline with discretion to move up to 15 percent above or below the policy weights. There were no real estate investments or foreign securities in the three balanced portfolios. Also, the fixed-income components of the three portfolios were relatively short. Consequently, there existed a considerable disparity between the management pension committee's policy asset mix decision and the actual fund mix.

Out of these realities, the Vice President, pension asset management began to build a three-phase implementation plan. The first order of priority would be to get the fund asset mix more closely alligned with the recently taken asset mix policy decisions.

TABLE 6-5 Passive/Value-Added Split for Fund Recommended by Consultant

	Passive Allocation ($ millions)	Value-added Allocations ($ millions)	
Permanent risk capital:			
Domestic stocks	$215	5 × $25	= $125
Real estate	$245	4 × $20	= $ 80
Small business	0	10 × $ 6.5	= $ 65
Foreign securities	$145	2 × $25	= $ 50
Permanent debt capital:			
Long bonds	$275	0	
Shift account			
Stocks/bonds/T-bills	0	2 × $50	= $100
Totals	$880		$420
Percent of fund	68%		32%

Secondly, a start would be made on installing an explicit value-added dimension in ALPHA's pension investment program. Third, an internal asset management capability would be created with a passive, cost-minimizing focus. Meanwhile, the value-added dimension would be expanded at a realistic rate, taking resource constraints—especially time—into account.

To effectively communicate the plan to the management pension committee, the pension asset manager constructed a number of pictures. Figure 6-1 uses the consultant's two-dimensional structure matrix to summarize the current status of ALPHA's pension assets.

In discussing the current situation, the VP-pension asset management made a number of important observations. First, the current ALPHA-investment manager relationships suffer from the malaise described by the consultant. The current three traditional managers believe they have a mandate that stresses risk control with investment value-added only a secondary consideration. Based on a study of past communications between ALPHA and the three managers, ALPHA's new pension asset manager suggested that the traditional managers had probably interpreted their mandates correctly.

All three managers run highly diversified large capitalization stock portfolios and high-grade medium-term bond portfolios. The portfolio cash positions have historically varied from a low of 5 percent to a high of 15 percent. No explicit distinction between passive and value-added components exists in the portfolios. In aggregate, ALPHA's pension fund has produced a return close to the median of other pension funds of similar size and similar asset mixes.

FIGURE 6-1 Current Structure and Dollar Allocation ($ billions)

	Passive Management	Value-Added Management
Internal Management	$0	$0
External Management	$1.1 (?)	$0.2 (?)

Second, the fund currently has little or no exposure to long duration bonds, foreign securities, real estate, or small business investments. Consequently, it is at odds with the recently established asset mix policy for the fund.

Third, it would be difficult to implement any significant change from the present structure for administrative reasons. All three current investment managers provided their own custodial and reporting services. ALPHA's senior managers were personal trustees of the fund. This combination provided an inappropriate legal and administrative structure from which to build the hybrid investment structure envisaged.

These realities formed the basis of a three-phase plan for transforming ALPHA's pension investment program.

A Three-Phase Transformation Plan

The VP-pension asset management informed the management pension committee that action on phase I would commence immediately. This phase consisted of three sequential steps. They are summarized in Table 6-6.

In commenting on phase I, the VP-pension asset management stated the belief that maintaining good relations with the three current investment managers was critically important. This meant full disclosure of

---

TABLE 6-6 Transformation Plan: Phase I

---

1. **Current Managers:** Inform them of ALPHA's plans. Tell them they are potential candidates for any "Outside Agent" position where they offer a service ALPHA needs. Estimate the size and timing of moneys required from them to fund new fund investment dimensions.
2. A **Single Master Custodian/Trustee:** Commence an immediate search for an organization that can meet the new security custody, information, and related needs of the pension investment program.
3. **New Asset Classes:** Create passive positions in long bonds ($200 million), real estate ($200 million), and foreign securities ($100 million).

ALPHA's plans and evenhanded treatment as they were being implemented.

A single, state-of-the-art, master trustee meant a quantum leap in effiencies, ranging from pension system cash management, to single source unitized accounting, to on-line access to the fund and its components. With this access went an array of software packages capable of analyzing the fund's portfolio characteristics and investment performance. The latter features would become useful in monitoring and controlling the investment program once it was operational.

With such a master trustee service in place, establishing the passive bond, real estate, and foreign security positions could occur very quickly. By buying zero-coupon long government bonds with durations in excess of 20 years, no ongoing management would be required until some time in the future when the position might require some lengthening of term.

A number of reputable international money managers were qualified to passively invest the initial $100 million designated for foreign investments with very little implementation lag. The passive real estate program might take longer to implement, but the considerable number of large open-end pooled funds in operation today could absorb ALPHA's designated $200 million over a period of time.[2]

Phase II would start the process of building value-added investment programs for ALPHA's pension fund. There were two obvious areas that would get attention first: domestic stocks and the asset shift account. Over $200 million is destined to go into these two areas. In phase II, one goal is to establish a five sub portfolio domestic stocks component (allocation would be ideally $20 to $30 million per manager). The other goal is to establish a two-part asset mix shift component with $50 million per manager.

FIGURE 6-2 Ultimate Structure and Dollar Allocation ($ billions)

	Passive	Value-Added
Internal	$0.2 to $0.4	$0
External	$0.3 to $0.4	$0.8 to $0.5

Phase II could formally commence soon after phase I ended. Indeed, the process of writing job effectiveness descriptions could be done in parallel with phase I activities. Also, the process of narrowing down the eligible universe of candidates for the two types of positions to a manageable "for discussion" candidate list could take place parallel to phase I. An outside consultant would be engaged to provide support in performing both tasks.[3]

Phase III would advance and consolidate the value-added dimension of the overall fund investment program. In addition, the shape and nature of any internal investment management function would be decided as part of this phase. While it was impossible to be precise at this point the steady state structure matrix might look like Figure 6-2.

In percentage terms, the numbers imply a 40–60 to 60–40 split between explicitly passive money and explicitly value-added money. Most of the fund is visualized as being managed outside in the final steady state mode. The VP-pension asset management noted that if the "value added" components could on average produce a 2 percent per annum net increment, a overall fund increment of 1 percent per annum becomes a viable target.

On the subject of resource needs for the asset management function, its manager did not foresee any involving significant dollar outlays in the first year of operation. In all likelihood, only two internal people would be required in addition to the manager to run the business in its first year of operation. A second professional was needed to act as backup to the manager. The first major challenge for this individual would be to work with the new master custodian to set up the required administrative and control procedures for the asset management function.

A second responsibility area for the second professional was the development or acquisition of planning tools. These tools would support the advisory role the pension asset management team had in relation to the management pension committee. A computer model that could provide pension system asset and liability values based on a variety of economic assumptions is a good example of this type of tool.

The third person would have an administrative assistant role in the group. Because an electronic work environment was envisaged for the asset management operation, this third person would have to be effective working in this type of environment.

The other major first-year resource would be an outside consultant to be engaged on a project-by-project basis. The key ingredients this outside resource would supply were information and insight gained through practical experience working with pension asset managers. Which master custodial systems could potentially meet our specifications? Is there anything we should know about the suppliers that might be less than obvious?

Which open-end pooled real estate funds meet the diversification and fee level criteria we have set for the passive real estate program? Which 20 domestic stock specialists best fit a given profile for successful value-added management? How many money management firms are out there that could psychologically handle an aggressive market timing mandate involving the taking of large "bets" for or against the stock, bond, or cash markets? Or should it be a computer program?

While the detailed numbers had yet to be done, the VP-pension asset management envisaged coming in with an internal cost budget—including all external fees other than for master trustee and investment management services—under $400,000. In relation to a $1.3 billion pension fund, this sum represents about 3 basis points.

Aggregate fund custodial and investment management fees need be no higher than the current 30 basis points (close to $4 million) cost. The installation of multimanager value-added investment programs would increase fees. However, these increases would be offset by fee reductions on the fund components going explicitly passive. There would be no management fee at all on the $200 million zero-coupon bond position, for example. Also, modern master trustee services, such as crediting interest on all fund cash balances and security lending, would further help control costs.

TABLE 6-7   An Investment Manager Job Description: The Domestic Stock Specialist Position

Plan Sponsor:	
Investment Manager:	
Effective Contract Date:	
Fund Investment Component to Be Managed:	Value-added management within the domestic stocks component of the fund.
Role of Component in Overall Fund Asset Mix Policy:	Part of the fund's permanent position in equity investments.
Manager Mandate:	The manager will have full discretion to manage part of the common stock component of the company's pension fund, subject to the following guidelines: • No securities issued by ALPHA Corporation may be held. • No foreign securities may be held. • No more than 10 percent of the portfolio may be in securities other than domestic common stocks. • The manager must be capable of demonstrating that all securities held in the portfolio are there primarily for money making rather than risk reduction reasons.
Performance Benchmark:	A passive portfolio with a composition to be jointly decided between the manager and the sponsor.
Performance Standards:	Successful management is deemed to be the outperformance of the benchmark portfolio by an average three percentage points per annum over moving four-year time frames.
Performance Tolerances:	The mandate can lead to considerable underperformance of the benchmark for short periods of time. Such underperformance could be up to 10 percentage points for one-year periods. Any time underperformance is more than this in any 12-month period or less, an accounting by the manager is expected.
Philosophy/Style:	The sponsor and the manager will agree on a set of portfolio characteristics (i.e., size of factor/industry group bets, number of names in the portfolio, portfolio turnover, etc.) that are consistent with the manager's investment philosophy/style. The manager will be prepared to explain any significant deviation from these characteristics.

TABLE 6-7 *(concluded)*

Personnel:	Any changes in status of the following key people will be reported to the sponsor immediately: Name Function
Reporting Requirements:	The following information will be communicated quarterly to the sponsor: • Month-end portfolio unit values. • A set of agreed-on portfolio characteristics. • Portfolio activity during the quarter, including purchases and sales, and brokerage by broker. • Investment intentions.
Termination:	Reasons for termination may include but are not limited to the following: • Not staying within investment mandate as per this agreement. • A loss of belief by the sponsor that the manager can achieve the performance standard as per this agreement (changes in key people, significant deviation from agreed-on portfolio characteristics, short-term portfolio performance outside established tolerances are events that could lead to this loss of belief).
Fees:	As agreed-on between the two parties. Any arrangement struck will be expected to be in place for at least two years.
Brokerage Allocation:	The manager is to execute all transactions so as to minimize their cost to the sponsor. No services other than pure execution are to be acquired for commissions.[4]

Implementing the Plan

Within months of discussing the implementation plan with the management committee, the VP-pension asset management brought phase I to a successful completion. The three existing traditional managers were informed about ALPHA's decisions. A master trustee that met the needs created by ALPHA's new approach to pension investing was engaged. The $200 million zero-coupon long bond position was created.

A manager was hired for the $100 million passive foreign securities position. Money had started to flow into highly diversified open-end pooled real estate funds in order to establish the passive real estate position. Internally, the three-person pension asset management team was busy learning how to work effectively with each other and with their electronic support equipment.

The commencement of the search for value-added managers marked the beginning of a new phase of the implementation plan. The pension asset management team worked hard to create job descriptions that would clearly convey the job they wanted done. The first one they tackled was for the domestic stocks specialist position. Table 6–7 shows the results of their labors.

Other job descriptions—for the asset mix shift positions, for the value-added positions in foreign securities, real estate, small business investments—followed. As months went by, the value-added dimension of ALPHA's pension investment program began to take shape.

The further ALPHA's Vice President, pension asset management got into the program, the more it became apparent that successful passive management was technique driven. Get the rules right and let computers execute. By contrast, successful value-added investment management was ultimately people—not technique—driven. Get the people right and let them make money their own way—but within your risk control structure. We will meet some of these people in the next chapter.

CHAPTER NOTES

1. The term *rented assets* was suggested to this author by Dean LeBaron, president of Batterymarch Financial Management. It fits the trusteed pension funds of defined benefit employer plans rather well. The money is legally owned by neither the shareholders nor the plan beneficiaries. It reverts to the beneficiaries only if the sponsor defaults on its pension debt.

    While the sponsor is not in default, it may use the assets to earn a return from which the shareholders are the beneficiaries. The higher the return, the lower its contribution rate needs to be to support any benefit promise. On the other hand, a poor investment return hurts the shareholders, not the plan beneficiaries. This risk is, in a sense, the rental fee.

2. As in a number of cases where implementability is assessed in relation to dollar amounts involved, situations are not identical in all national markets. Dealing with real estate funds specifically, Canada's open-end pools still aggregate to less than $1 billion, making ALPHA's $200 million look pretty formidable. The US equivalent is approaching $10 billion, which makes a $200 million sum look a lot smaller.

3. Is this the same consultant who did the policy work for ALPHA on the asset cushion size, the policy asset mix, and the investment management structure? It could be. But consulting practices can be value-adding and value-losing too. In the opinion of this writer, some—but by no means all—pension finance consultants have the mindset necessary to add value in assembling value-adding investment programs.

4. The ALPHA pension asset management team is coming down very clearly on the side of stock commissions representing an execution fee here. They are saying to prospective managers that they are not going to permit them to transfer manager operating costs—including investment research—to the pension fund through stock brokerage. See Chapter Nine, note 2 for further discussion on this issue.

CHAPTER SEVEN

Value-added Investment Professionals: Getting to Know Them

Do not summon people to your office—it frightens them. Instead, go see them in *their* offices.

—D. Ogilvy

The reader will now meet some almost real value-adding investment managers. By this I mean that the character sketches are based on real people, but there may not be an exact match between each character in this chapter and a single real person. The point of this chapter is that value-added investment management is often a highly individualistic pursuit. Finding good managers requires a prior understanding of what makes the good ones good.

MANAGEMENT BY WALKING AROUND

"Hands-on, value-driven" is one of the attributes of effective management touted by the writers of *In Search of Excellence.*[1] What form does this attribute take on when it is placed in a pension asset management context? In general terms, it means staying in touch with the people to whom functional responsibilities related to pension asset management have been delegated. In more specific terms, its application will vary depending on which function it is being applied to.

For the functions where there is a high task/system/process orientation—passive management, master trustee-custodial services—"staying in touch" means talking to technically oriented people about reducing costs, increasing system efficiencies, improving turnaround times, and so on. For value-added investment management, it means talking to money managers about their way of making money for the pension fund.

In the spirit of the Peters-Waterman book, such expressions as "walking around" and "staying in touch" are meant to convey actions that are of a positive rather than a negative nature. They should signal a genuine desire to learn, to understand, (and, in the process, even to have fun!) so that more informed decisions may be made. They should *not* be mistaken for a licence to second-guess specific decisions, to snoop, and to find fault.

Also, the expressions are not meant to suggest that a spirit of camaraderie should develop between plan sponsor representatives and money managers. The relationship is of a business not a social nature.

There is a likely generous return to those responsible for pension asset management from walking around. Such activity will lead to a deeper understanding of how outside service suppliers are going about the business of meeting the goals that have been jointly set with them.

This will, in turn, provide that needed extra dimension to assess the potential impact of material supplier changes—changes in ownership, in personnel, in technique—which will undoubtedly occur in the future. Such changes might or might not require action on the part of the plan sponsor. Either way, knowledgeable decisions will be better decisions.

Walking Around at ALPHA Corporation

ALPHA's Vice President, pension asset management was an active practicioner of the hands-on style of management. This meant developing more than just a read-the-brochure and formal-interview level of knowledge and understanding of the investment management team that was in the process of being assembled.

The VP has just returned from a series of drop-in visits with some of the new managers. Each visit led to a lasting impression of the individual visited and his or her working environment. While each individual was unique in many ways, the ALPHA pension assets manager had been struck by the ease with which they could be fitted into one of a number of categories. The categories were the VP's own; they were developed in the course of talking with and observing many managers over many years.

A type probably least likely to produce value-added over the long run is, ironically, the easiest to get to know and even to like. This is the comfort type. Gracious dinner companions, good listeners, good dressers, one got the feeling they viewed their job as being the buffer between the market and the client.

Their presentations laid a heavy stress on prudence, safety, and the depth and breadth of their oganizations. Despite their efforts to kick the habit, the future was often predicted by peeking in their rearview mirrors. Most are very nice people—the kind you would like as neighbors. None would get to manage any ALPHA pension assets.

The recluse type of manager is a great deal more difficult to get to know. Shyness or simply a lack of interest in becoming known make many of these managers unknowns. Consequently, it is very difficult to even find out how many managers of this type are out there.

Some gain noteriety despite themselves as they quietly pile up good results year after year through the steady application of usually simple investment rules. Warren Buffett is probably the best known recluse manager who has become famous in spite of himself.[2] The VP hoped ALPHA's search would uncover a few future Buffetts!

And then there was the extroverted you-can-quote-me type. The good ones have the same conviction about a specific way of making money that the good recluses do. They also have the same courage of their convictions as they follow through and execute money making ideas.

However, where the recluse type maybe seems smaller than life, the you-can-quote-me types are bigger than life. They will gladly sit down and tell you how they make money in the markets—for themselves, for you, for anybody with the intelligence to hire them as their money manager.

Where very few recluse types—even the good ones—end up managing a lot of money for a lot of clients, all the good you-can-quote-me types eventually do. To them, success is all-inclusive. It means not only making good investments but acknowledgment that good investments are being made.

The most convincing acknowledgment is to be given new money to manage by new, large, knowledgeable clients. In the process, another type of success starts to unfold. Asset value-based fees push the investment firm's revenues higher and higher while costs stay fixed.

ALPHA's VP, pension asset management observed that this almost certain evolution creates a potential problem for clients looking for value-added management from this type of manager. Commercial success in a money management firm can lead to a slow change in style, as more and more money and clients with different needs must be accommodated.

How, the value-added searcher might legitimately ask, can we continue to get pure, uncompromised value-added management under these circumstances? It was a question the VP had been most anxious to answer. ALPHA's talent search had led to a number of managers falling into this category.

One of these firms was under consideration for one of the domestic stocks mandate positions. Fortunately, an informal visit with Chris, one of the key people in the firm, provided a possible answer.

Domestic Stocks: Buying Assets at a Discount

Chris falls into the extroverted, you-can-quote-me manager category. He and his associates have successfully applied a simple formula approach to investing their client's money for many years now. The formula is based on a view of the world stripped of all ambiguity. Investment opportunities come in bundles of assets, people that work those assets to make a profit, and markets into which products (made by the asset/people combination) are sold.

Out of these three dimensions, Chris and his associates have always focused on assets. The questions are always the same. At what price can we acquire assets through the stock markets? How does this price compare to our own estimate of the breakup value of the assets?

Ratios under 50 percent lead to purchases, ratios over 100 percent lead to sales. It's not that the other two dimensions—people and markets—do not matter. Markets, of course, must be factored into the breakup value calculation. As for people—corporate management specifically—well, if it is effective, fine. If it is not, it can be changed.

Consistent application of this approach over the years had produced good investment results for Chris and his associates. It had also brought them many new clients. Chris admitted that the investment and commercial success of their money management business was leading to a new, unwelcome business dimension.

Part of the client base, sometimes aided and abetted by their consultants, was exerting continuous pressure for good results if not every quarter, certainly every year. This pressure created a danger the firm might move away from its tried-and-true investment philosophy.

Chris explained that it had always been impossible to forecast when a convergence between their estimate of asset value and the market's estimate might occur. Very few occurred quickly. He could recall staying with a stock trading around $10 a share for four years. It did not move until the fifth year—but then it moved to over $100 a share.

With obvious delight, Chris showed ALPHA's pension asset manager his latest two money making ideas. Both research summaries were identically structured. The assets of the businesses—one a conglomerate, the other a major airline—were listed and valued. The market value of outstanding debt was subtracted. (The VP, pension asset management had approvingly noted pensions assets, and debt had been properly accounted for!)

The resulting net asset values were divided by the number of shares outstanding. In both cases, the resulting net asset value per share approximated twice the quoted share value on the stock exchange. Both companies qualified as acquisition candidates.

When and how might Chris' price and the market price converge? That, of course, was the great unknown. Maybe tomorrow, maybe next year, maybe in five years, maybe never. "What I do to make money is not much different from what real estate specialists and venture capital specialists do to make money," said Chris. "Yet plan sponsors will give them 5 to 10-year money with only progress reports expected on the way through. More and more of my clients put me under a microscope every quarter. It's counterproductive!"

This complaint triggered an idea in the VP's mind. How would Chris and his associates feel about running $25 million of ALPHA domestic stocks money using a typical direct asset investment arrangement? For example, the $25 million could be put under Chris' control for, say, a fixed, five-year period.

Chris would have full discretion during this period to buy assets at a discount of 50 percent or more from their estimated value. He could sell such acquisitions at any time deemed appropriate. He would be expected to return the terminal value of the portfolio in cash to ALPHA five years hence.

On the fee side, it would be structured the same way as a venture fund. A fixed fee would be struck to help pay the overhead. A participation fee would be struck based on the success of the investment program over the five-year horizon. The entrepreneurial side of Chris wanted to immediately, say "Yes, let's work out the details." However, his practical side—which required that this idea be thoroughly discussed first with his associates—prevailed.

ALPHA's Vice President, pension asset management awaited their response with interest.

"Hands-On" Management in Real Estate

When ALPHA's pension asset manager called up Stephen, partner in one of the recently hired real estate investment firms, to make a request, the response was almost instantaneous. Would it be possible to sometime spend a day with Stephen to get closer to the real estate investment process? "I'll pick you up at 6 tomorrow morning," was the response. "My day will go until 8 tomorrow night. You're welcome to be along for part of my day or for the duration."

By 6:30 the following morning a bleary-eyed VP-pension asset management was walking around a building already in Stephen's portfolio. It turned out that it was not the small office building itself that would be the center of attention but the supermarket and its parking lot next door.

Stephen had received word through his network of contacts that a grocery chain was going to sell the store adjacent to "his" property. (While properties were under Stephen's control, he talked as though he owned them.) If the chain was really selling, a potential opportunity to expand and redevelop the property existed, including the ability to offer generous parking facilities to current and new lessees.

Stephen declared the concept probably workable if the adjacent property could be acquired for under $2 million. Next step: find out through a trusted third party if the property was indeed going up for sale and, if so, at what price. After a quick breakfast, Stephen moved on to what would turn out to be the "coup" of the day, if not the week or even month.

For weeks he had had his eye on a rundown but extremely well-located owner occupied office building. The building had been put up for sale by the owners but at a higher price than Stephen wanted to pay. The owners wanted to move into modern leased quarters, ideally close to their previous location.

Stephen happened to have two floors available in a recently refurbished office building close to the building for sale. A few days ago, he had asked his "numbers man" to work out a lease which, were the vendors to sign it, would permit Stephen to buy the vendor's building at their price.

The idea was to make up the too-high purchase price on their building with lease terms favorable to Stephen, the lessor of the two floors—who also would be the building purchaser. Both the property to be bought and the space to be leased would be and were in ALPHA's real estate portfolio, avoiding any conflict in how to allocate the "loss" and offsetting "gain."

By 8:30, Stephen and the (now somewhat more awake) VP were sitting with the "numbers man." He showed them a lease that, assuming the vendor's building would to into the portfolio at the asking price, would accomplish the goal of effectively reducing the acquisition cost through its favorable (to the lessor) terms. The numbers worked, and the deal would be presented that afternoon.

Nine o'clock marked the beginning of the regular weekly investment committee meeting. During the next two hours Stephen and his associates reviewed and made decisions on 14 projects that had passed their initial screen as potential purchase candidates, 7 where offers were outstanding, and two where offers had been accepted but had not yet closed.

The rest of the day continued at this pace. Late in the afternoon, while Stephen was reading the riot act to an agent he believed to be creating a false market in downtown commercial space,[3] the word came that the owner-occupiers had accepted the joint purchase/lease offer.

After a moment's celebration, it was off to the closing of a deal struck last month. After that—well, ALPHA's VP-pension asset management had to stop into the ALPHA offices for a little while—did Stephen mind carrying on on his own? With a quick handshake and smile, Stephen was off. There was much yet to be done before he would permit himself to call it a day.

ALPHA's pension assets manager was struck by the similarities and differences in Chris' and Stephen's approach to making money for the ALPHA pension fund. Both were attempting to buy assets at bargain prices. However, once bought, Stephen went on to manage the assets for a number of years, an activity Chris almost always[4] left to others.

The Small Business Connection

If Chris and Stephen were first and foremost asset buyers, Tim was a buyer of people-idea packages first, with assets a secondary consideration. ALPHA's pension fund VP had spent a lot of time with Tim before deciding to participate in his firm's small business capital fund. There was an important psychological barrier to be broken before committing pension trust assets to the small business area. The VP's was breached only after a long informal talk with Tim.

It takes some getting used to the idea that out of every dollar invested into this area, 20 cents will have to be written off completely and a further 20 cents might only pay back 10 cents—with the other 10 cents having to be written off. Not only that, but these writeoffs tend to come early in the life of the fund. The bad news comes fast; the good news only comes much later. Is it fiduciarily responsible to subject pension fund money to this kind of experience?

The answer can be yes, the VP decided, as long as two conditions hold. First, overall fund asset mix policy must be responsibly determined—as it had been in ALPHA's case. That would ensure that no single asset class could derail the overall fund investment program. Second, the small business investment program must be responsibly executed. The talk with Tim had helped the VP understand more clearly what that second condition really meant.

It was really very simple. In no other investment area is diversification more important. With only three out of five investments likely to make any money, material downside protection can only be achieved by having many eggs in many baskets.

But diversification alone is not enough. Each project going into the fund (out of the hundreds that were looked at) must have a good shot at a longer term-return over 20–25 percent per year. That is where Tim and his associates came in. It requires a rare blend of patience, maturity, toughness, and business savvy to assemble a portfolio with these characteristics.

Only through discussions with Tim had the VP come to appreciate that finding an attractive investment opportunity was only the beginning of the investment process. Good entrepreneurs don't easily part with 20 percent to 40 percent of the equity of a business and possibly more if performance targets are not met. Tim asserted that it was here that many a potentially good deal had died. This was especially so during periods when alternative sources of funds—from the banks, from government agencies—were readily available.

Tim had talked about the role of the "competition" with some bitterness. He did not think it responsible behavior on the part of some banks to load entrepreneurs up with floating-rate debt when it was really equity money they needed. The problem with well-meaning civil servants handing out grants or soft loans was that no proprietary interest situation was created. When Tim put money on the line, part of it—even if only a few pennies for each dollar—was his own.[5] It meant a bonding of sorts—for better or for worse.

Refreshingly, Tim had openly talked about the "for-worse" side of the business. Just the day before, he had flown to the West Coast to shut down a venture. Sales had been coming in well below projections on a product that had looked like a sure-fire winner.

Inventories were piling up. No buyers could be found for either the business or the inventories. Tim said that this had been the toughest part of the business to learn. Telling an entrepreneur (and his wife and maybe even his kids) that it was all over would never be easy. It comes, nevertheless, with the territory.

Tim was looking forward to getting the startup phase for this particular fund behind him. In a few years, the 10-times-your-money investments would start to surface. Did Tim want to guess which ones they would be? His answer was instructive.

He felt very bullish about another West Coast situation where he had recommended a 50 percent writedown of their original investment only six months ago. A new management team had been given a mandate to turn the project around. As of last week, it looked like they would not only meet the sales and profitability goals in the original business plan, but would in fact surpass them by a wide margin!

The VP-pension asset management decided to touch base with Tim at least once or twice a year—for not one, but two, reasons. Progress with the investment fund was of obvious interest. But there was also a window here for the managers of ALPHA Corporation's other businesses.

The knowledge and information base Tim and his associates needed to conduct their business could on occasion be very useful to ALPHA in managing its own businesses. ALPHA's pension assets manager decided to be an informal conduit between the two.

Going International

A conversation with Constance had taken out some of the romance the VP had associated with investing pension money outside the country. The 100 or so investment firms now soliciting pension fund money for investment in foreign markets seemed capable of being categorized into the same style categories as domestic managers. Some emphasized growth, others value, still others market timing across different national markets.

It was Constance's belief that this growing pool of "free-to-roam" money was also creating more and more homogeneity in the way assets were being valued in national capital markets. Segmented markets with potentially unique opportunities for outsiders were giving way to more integrated markets with prices determined not by just domestic participants, but by outsiders as well.[6]

Having made these general observations, the president of one of ALPHA's international specialist organizations began to talk with relish about the still many exceptions to the general trend. It was a mistake to treat the European Economic Community as one economic and financial entity.

The mindset the British and French brought to their respective capital markets had always been different and probably always would be. The phenomenal Japanese savings rate would probably always lead to their capital asset prices being higher than elsewhere. And there would always be new markets to open up.

Constance had just returned from one of the small, dynamic Pacific Rim economies. There she had negotiated permission from national authorities to buy $50 million of the common shares of domestic corporations. The vehicle would be a closed-end fund with Contance's clients putting up the $50 million. The money would be invested by a government-approved local investment advisor with the investment mandate established by Constance's firm.

Why was she so excited about this new vehicle's prospects? Well, remember what happened in Japan. At one time, stocks in Japan sold at four times earnings while the economy moved ahead at a phenomenal rate of growth. Yes there was tremendous market volatility, but that is to be expected in any young, still maturing capital market. Where is the Japanese market today? Much higher multiples, much less volatility.

This smaller economy is today where Japan was 20 years ago, said Constance. The economy is growing fast, stocks are selling at three, four, five times earnings. No doubt there is risk. Economic risk, political risk. The market volatility is twice, three times that of the Japanese market. But with the political direction in which Red China seems to be heading, the prospects for growth and stability at the other side of the Pacific look very promising.

ALPHA Corporations's Vice President, pension asset management was intrigued with the prospect of ALPHA's pension fund being among the first foreign buyers of shares in this domestic market. If the experience came even close to matching that of early investors in the Japanese market, value would indeed be added to ALPHA's pension fund results.

Markets as Investments

It was with some surprise that ALPHA's pension asset manager had come to realize that asset shift managers are a breed apart from other investment professionals. Sure, all investment professionals talk about the markets. Most have some views about what future events might influence the course of stock prices and interest rates. But very few have chosen to build their investment practice on anticipating the course of stock prices and interest rates and aggressively shifting their portfolios in line with these anticipations.

Out of all the visits with the external value-added managers, the visit with John had been the only one that had left the VP with a lingering sense of disquiet. Not that John and his three associates were not highly competent. It was a matter of admitting that the decision to allocate $50 million to them was more of an act of faith than it had been with the others.

This was so despite the calm confidence with which John talked about the dynamics of public sector financial management in a democratic society. About how it naturally tended to excesses, giving rise to major swings in the yield curve around a basically upward bias.

John also implied, without actually saying so, that he could profit from the group think behavior of the other money managers. The others talked contrarily; John actually bought their securities when they didn't want to own them and sold them back when this psychology had reversed itself.

Another vaguely disturbing thing to the VP about this style of money management was its devastating simplicity. The psychological "home" position is 100 percent in T-bills. Occasional forays are made from homebase into the bond and stock markets. The forays are executed by buying only the most liquid bonds or stocks—or futures contracts if more advantageous. Positions are held until one of two things happens. Prices change, or your perception of the environment changes.

This simplicity carried over into the offices of John and his associates. While there were a few separate meeting areas, all investment activity took place in "the room." There, the four investment professionals faced each other and a battery of screens and telephones.

A continuous information flow was coolly observed, analyzed, and discussed. Day after day, week after week, month after month. And the use of it all? To pull the trigger one day and move from one investment posture to another, often in a matter of hours.

The toughest part of being an asset shift specialist? No, it is not making the decision to blow out the T-bills and buy the long bond or the stock market, said John. It is the decision to stay with the T-bills while these markets mount a false (you hope) rally. Collecting handsome management fees while sitting in T-bills when the stocks and bonds are rising used to cause considerable discomfort.

"But not any more?" asked the VP. John replied that his client base had pretty well gotten used to occasionally being in that uncomfortable position. Any client who had had assets with the firm for any period longer than four years had made money in the sense of doing better than T-bills, long bonds, or stocks as measured by broad market indices.

As a result, the firm's portfolios are outperformed 95 percent of a large sample of pension funds for periods in excess of four years. (The VP knew this to be a fact from the research done for ALPHA by the outside consultant last year).

While the style required to execute successfully an asset mix shift account left the VP somewhat uneasy, comfort could be derived from two factors. First, John and his associates had the mandate and the mental toughness to immediately implement their market judgments. They would do, not just talk. Second, they have less than 5 percent of AL-PHA's pension assets to work with. A wrong call would not have a major impact at the total fund level.

Staying in Touch with the Fund

The most vivid image that remained with ALPHA's pension asset manager from Sally's guided tour was actually seeing the fund live on a computer terminal screen. Sally was vice president in charge of master trustee services at one of the nation's largest financial institutions. The purpose of the tour had been to get a first-hand look at the new developments recently announced by the master trustee services group.

The striking thing about seeing the fund had been how current its status had been. Only a few years ago, monthly updates were the norm. Now the norm was on-line access. Asset holdings and weightings, cash balances, transaction activity, pending purchases and sales as of right now were displayed on the screen—by investment manager, by component, and at the total fund level.

Sally had explained the whole new range of services made possible by this live, real-time environment. Idle pension fund cash balances (once a great boon to the banking side of the financial institution) were now a thing of the past. Regular electronic sweeps now scooped up any cash balance found and paid a competitive rate on it. The lending of the fund's securities to investment dealers had also become a new source of revenues for the fund.

The provision of computer-based passive management services was another natural extension of the new real-time computer environment. Implementation routines for any of a number of passive stock or bond investment strategies were available to clients.[7]

The most recent series of innovations had focused on reporting investment return for the fund and its components. Sally explained that frequent fund valuations permitted frequent unit value calculations. Frequent unit value calculations permitted more accurate rates of return calculations. Such calculations could be performed by manager, by fund component, or by any aggregation thereof, right up to the total fund level.[8]

She went on to explain that any manager or component return calculation could be accompanied by a benchmark return calculation, with the benchmark to be specified by the user. At an even more sophisticated level, multiple benchmarks could be used to understand where any return differentials—between fund components and the selected benchmarks—were coming from.[9]

The VP-pension asset management made a mental note to get back to Sally on the this topic. The pension asset management group had been working on its internal fund control system for some time now. The design was almost finished. It appeared that Sally's master trustee system was capable of feeding the internal control system with most of the inputs it would need.

The VP marveled at how, in only a few years, the old package of legal, custodial, recordkeeping, and reporting services offered by virtually all major financial institutions had been transformed.

Master trustee services had become a highly competitive, highly specialized field. The high development costs required to stay competitive had already forced a number of institutions out of this market. More would likely follow. Meanwhile, the few leaders continued to pour money into systems and into people like Sally and her colleagues. Having taken the lead, they seemed determined to keep it.

But Just Walking Around Is Not Enough

ALPHA's pension assets manager was pleased with what had been accomplished through the visits. Closer understandings had been forged; new ideas had resulted. The regular walk-arounds would continue.

But important as the qualitative control dimension is, it is not enough. Multibillion-dollar businesses must also have a quantitative control dimension. Creating it had been a high-priority project for ALPHA's pension assets management team. Work on it was ending. The Vice President, pension asset management was anxious to unveil the information system that would play a critical role in controlling the $1.3 billion pension fund.

CHAPTER NOTES

1. Thomas J. Peters and Robert H. Waterman, *In Search of Excellence,* Harper & Row, 1982.

2. Despite many enticements, this legendary investor never did leave Omaha, Nebraska. An ardent disciple of the Ben Graham school of security valuation, Buffett's energies in recent years have been going into his own holding company, Berkshire Hathaway. According to Peter Bernstein, reading the annual reports of Berkshire Hathaway "is an excellent substitute for attending Harvard Business School."

3. A "false market" in the real estate business is agent-originated activity that has clients moving between buildings, taking advantage of rental inducements. The agents win by collecting their commissions on all such moves. False markets thrive when vacancy rates rise, unless controlled by real estate managers.

4. Some common stock portfolio managers do take more than just a passing interest in the management of companies in which they have invested. However, active involvement in the management of a company's affairs continues to be the exception rather than the rule. By contrast, hands-on real estate portfolio management invariably means physical property management.

5. A 1 percent to 2 percent management fee and a 20 percent carry of fund profits is a standard arrangement. In addition, the general partner—that is, the venture capital specialist—puts up some of the firm's own capital to be invested alongside the money put up by the pension funds.

6. Considerable literature now exists on some of the unique dimensions of international investing. Some of it has been collected, edited, and published in *International Investing* , edited by Peter L. Bernstein, Institutional Investor Books, 1983.

7. These strategies on the stock side could be based on replicating the results of broad market indices, such as the Standard and Poor's 500 Stock Index in the United States and the Toronto Stock Exchange 300 Stock Index in Canada. Variations on this basic theme result from systematically "tilting" away from some of the fundamental characteristics of these broad market indices.

    The most popular of these tilts is toward a proportionately higher weighting in smaller capitalization stocks. Tilts toward low price-earnings ratio stocks and high-yield stocks are also popular. In all cases, the idea is to boost long-term return by holding stocks whose common characteristics appear to have resulted (and hopefully will continue to do so) in an extra margin of return.

    On the bond side, passive strategies tend to be related to matching projected pension system outflows. We discussed their place in the financial management of pension systems at some length in Chapter Three—the chapter on asset cushion policy for the pension system.

8. The unit value concept has, of course, been around for decades in the mutual fund business. It is the price at which fund inflows buy into the fund and at which fund outflows cash out. Powerful computers permit these calculations to take place not only at the total fund level, but also at the fund component, subcomponent, and even sub subcomponent levels. The result is an ability to calculate rates of return at whatever level of fund disaggregation or aggregation is desired.

9. The rationale for these multiple benchmarks comes from findings during the 1970s that security prices seem to move in tandem or independently, depending on how much of certain characteristics they have in common. These characteristics have been described in differing but related ways by leading finance and investment theorists such as Richard Roll, Barr Rosenberg, and William Sharpe.

    The general idea is that, within the security markets, individual securities are priced according to the characteristics of the securities themselves and those of their issuers. Many securities and issuers have characteristics in common with other securities and issuers.

    The result is that, in pricing securities, there ought to exist relationships related to these common characteristics. Also, a good deal of after-the-fact price behavior ought to be explainable by reference to the characteristics.

    In the stock area, such characteristics might be company size, earnings growth and variability, earnings sensitivity to such external forces as the inflation rate, the ratio of stock price to earning and dividends, and financial leverage. For bonds, they might be duration, quality of the issuer, and any options attached to the instrument—exercisable by either the issuer or the bondholder.

    The attribution of portfolio or portfolio component returns to exposure (or lack of it) to these characteristics could help explain why returns were what they were. What you do once the attribution exercise is completed is another matter. This question will be addressed in Chapter Eight.

PART FOUR

Control

Control: From Information to Judgment

If we did not do this already, would we—knowing what we now know—go into it?

—P. Drucker

A pension plan information system must be capable of doing two things: It must be capable of calculating plan assets and liabilities on a best estimate basis. It must also be capable of measuring the contribution the pension fund is making to the bottom line of the plan sponsor.

The first capability is needed to assess the size of the asset cushion and thus the solvency of the plan. The second capability recognizes the fund as a potential contributor to corporate profitability. Fund contributions to corporate profitability can come from three sources: the capital markets through the risk-free interest rate, the fund asset mix policy, and the fund investment management program. The information system must distinguish between these three sources.

This chapter builds the plan information system and discusses its uses and limitations. The system's major limitation, of course, is that it is only an information system. It cannot automatically convert information to judgments and decisions. Only people can do that.

CONTROL SYSTEMS AND CONTROL SYSTEMS

The business of providing retirement benefits to employees requires not one but two control systems—just like other financial businesses such as banking and insurance. One such system meets the needs of outside regulators charged with ensuring promised benefits are indeed paid and that no one profits dishonestly in the process.[1]

Sadly, little of the data and reports required for regulatory compliance is of much use to those responsible for actually managing the pension business. Thus, while the regulators might be satisfied with a control system that focuses on the enforcement of external rules and regulations, such a system is unlikely to meet internal needs. Internal control needs flow from monitoring progress towards achieving internally set goals.

Are targets being met? If not, why not? Is a need for change indicated? Paraphrasing Peter Drucker,[2] if we could make last year's decisions over again, would they be the same? What is the cost of changing our minds? What is the cost of *not* changing our minds? This chapter addresses control from the perspective of these questions.

If the primary goal of the pension fund is to secure the employer's promise to make benefit payments in the future, an important control system requirement has been identified. Those with the responsibility for meeting this goal need an information system capable of estimating comparable values of pension assets and liabilities at regular frequencies.

With such estimates, the value of the asset cushion in the pension system (that is, the difference between the asset and liability estimates) can be monitored regularly over time. As long as this asset cushion is positive, the pension fund is achieving its primary goal.

A legitimate secondary goal is to achieve the primary goal at minimum cost to the corporation. To monitor progress toward this secondary goal, the information system must be capable of attributing changes in the value of the pension fund to specific causes. These causes will fall into one of four categories. They will be new money-related, investment management-related, asset mix policy-related, or risk-free return-related.

Thus, an effective pension management information system must be capable of doing two fundamental things. It must be capable of monitoring the size of the plan asset cushion. And it must be capable of measuring the contribution the pension fund is making to reducing the cost of the pension system to its sponsor. Part of this second capability should be the attribution of this contribution to investment operations, to investment policy decisions, and to the prevailing real interest rate environment.

The Pension Balance Sheet: A Focal Point for the Control System

The balance sheet is an excellent focal point for the pension management information system. From its vantage point, all of the action taking place in the system can be seen. Figure 8–1 shows the balance sheet and the factors that will lead to changes in the dollar value of its components.

The regular estimation of pension assets and liabilities is a totally feasible proposition today. We saw in the previous chapter that a modern portfolio information system will supply almost real-time asset values, with only direct investments in real estate and small business subject to any significant estimation error.

We made reference to the availability of microcomputer-based pension liability estimation software in Chapter Three. This software, when supplied with data on the plan member population, will calculate a pension liability for a set of economic best estimates—fund return, wage and price inflation—in a matter of minutes if not seconds.

Sources of Change in Value of Pension Liabilities

A regular asset and liability estimation routine would likely indicate that the growth in pension liabilities is quite predictable most of the

---

FIGURE 8-1   Pension Balance Sheet Changes: Control
System Focal Point

Asset Value Change	Liability Value Change

Impact of:
    Contributions?
    Risk free return?
    Asset mix policy?
    Investment operations?
	Impact of:
	    Normal factors?
	    (actual experience over period)
	    Special factors?
	    (changes in plan benefits,
	    changes in economic best
	    estimates)

	Asset Cushion Value Change Asset Value Change minus Liability Value Change

time. However, there are special circumstances that could create an occasional liability swing of major proportions.

Such swings will invariably come from one of two sources. A change in economic best estimates—the fund investment rate and the wage/price inflation rate—would do it. A material change in benefits policy—promising postretirment inflation protection in the plan text, for example—would also do it.

But benefits policy changes will likely be very infrequent and hence will not often contribute to a liability change explanation. Best estimate economic assumptions will change from period to period. This is so because interest rates change continuously. But changes in interest rates by themselves should only have a muted effect on economic assumption changes. Only a material change in the gap between interest rates and inflation for an extended period of time will lead to a material change in the value of pension liabilities.[3]

Thus, period-to-period changes in the minimum dollar requirement (i.e., the best estimate of the going-concern accrued pension liability) are—with the exceptions noted—not likely to be major contributors to random period-to-period changes in the plan asset cushion. Such changes are more likely to come from the asset side of the balance sheet.

Sources of Change in Value of the Pension Assets

The concept of a minimum risk asset mix policy was studied in the asset mix policy chapter (Chapter Four). The intent of this policy is to create the closest match possible between the duration and inflation-sensitivity of the pension assets and the pension liabilities.

The risk-minimization theme can be extended in how the policy is implemented. It implies the use of high-grade securities and a passive investment management style. These policies together will produce a close correlation between plan asset and liability value fluctuations over time. As a result, the asset cushion should not fluctuate greatly over time.

In the course of defining the minimum risk investment policy, the two major sources of asset-side asset cushion variability become apparent. One is asset mix policy; the other is its implementation through investment operations.

It is absolutely essential to keep the impact of these two factors on the size of the asset cushion separate. As we saw in the implementation chapter (Chapter Six), responsibility for asset mix policy and responsibility for its actual implementation through investment operations are likely to rest in quite different places.

FIGURE 8-2 The Pension Fund Return
Decomposition Needed for Effective
Managerial Control

Return component due to:
Risk-free return	X%
Asset mix policy	Y%
Investment operations	Z%
Total fund return	X% + Y% + Z%

A basic three-part decomposition of pension fund return is suggested by this discussion. For any measurement period, total fund return breaks down into components due to the risk-free return provided by the capital markets, due to the fund's chosen asset mix policy, and due to the results of the fund's investment management program. Figure 8-2 shows this breakdown schematically.[4]

It is impossible to make any qualitative judgments about pension fund performance without knowing how total fund return breaks down into these three components. Yet they are seldom calculated in actual practice. No wonder there is so much collective chest beating when fund performance is good (everyone is responsible) and finger pointing when the results are bad (someone else is responsible)!

The decomposition of performance into captial market, asset mix policy, and investment operations components can be the start of much more useful discussions of what fund performance has been and if any change in policies or personnel is indicated. But it is only the start. Having the right information cannot by itself answer Peter Drucker's question. Bad results must be understood, but they do not automatically call for change. So it is with good results. They do not automatically signal a stay pat position.

From Information to Judgment

Demand and supply conditions in the capital markets periodically create environments of low risk-free returns and of high risk-free returns. It is not very productive for plan sponsors to blame money managers for the low-return environments. Nor is it productive for money managers to take credit for the high-return environments. Good news or bad news from this source is beyond the control of either money manager or plan sponsor.

Yet such good news or bad news might well lead to decisions to adjust policies or even the investment management structure. A growing asset cushion, for example, might lead to the justification of a more aggressive asset mix policy stance or even a more aggressive investment management structure stance. A shrinking asset cushion might evoke the opposite response. This is a matter of judgment.

It is again capital market demand-supply conditions that determine what premiums end up being realized for the acceptance of equity risk, interest rate risk, and forgoing liquidity in any given period. The pension fund's basic exposure to these factors is determined by asset mix policy. Asset mix policy is part of corporate finance policy. Thus it is a senior management responsibility. Good news or bad news emanating from this source should not be attributed to the investment management function.

There is a more subtle point to be made about asset mix policy decisions. Should they ever be classified as being good or bad? They probably can be but not in the simplistic way that would make decisions leading to high returns good decisions and low-return decisions bad decisions.

Good decisions flow from understanding the longer-term good news–bad news prospects embodied in the capital markets—and from deciding on how much exposure to these prospects it is appropriate to subject the plan asset cushion to—and through it, the shareholders. In this sense, it is entirely possible that a good asset mix policy decision will periodically produce bad fund performance, not only absolutely—in the sense of low or even negative fund returns—but also relatively in relation to the performance of other pension funds. Journeys that end successfully are not necessarily uneventful while in progress.

Bad decisions result from ignoring long-term risk and reward considerations and instead engaging in the investment management activity we have called asset mix shifting. Once the plan sponsor board or senior management committees start confusing fundamental policy decisions and short-term fund investment decisions, all bets are off. Having said that, it is entirely possible that the absence of a soundly developed asset mix policy will not prevent a pension fund from achieving good investment results. This can be so in the same sense that a traveler can have an excellent journey—without knowing where the journey will lead.

Whatever decisions are made about asset mix policy, it is important to track their impact on fund performance. But again, what is done with this knowledge is ultimately a matter of judgment.

And so it is with investment management. Its impact on fund performance must be tracked. If the style is predominantly passive, little in the way of either good news or bad news should emanate from the monitoring system. The more the style is tilted to value-added management, the more scope results for positive or negative contributions to total fund return from this source. But should bad results lead to change? That is again a matter of judgment.

In fact, it is more a matter of judgment than most people think. Capital market efficiency is the reason why.

Capital Market Efficiency, Noise, and Signals

Quality control systems in many production processes benefit from having a high signal-to-noise ratio. The result is that, when something goes awry, it is quickly discovered and corrected. Thus a cookie baker would probably be quickly alerted or problems such as cookies that were too small, or too big, or underbaked, or overbaked. Often a simple adjustment—to the cookie cutter, to the oven—will fix the problem.

Value-added investment management is not a production process with a high signal-to-noise ratio. In fact, it suffers from a very low signal-to-noise ratio. Thus even the most finely tuned quality control system here will produce mainly random noises rather than action-oriented signals. This problem is shown graphically in Figure 8-3.

The reason for the low signal-to-noise ratio coming out of the investment management control monitor? Recall the investment structure discussions of Chapter Five. We argued there that the material risk in electing to go with value-added management was not the extra return volatility it might produce, but that it might not deliver value-added. We called this risk manager selection risk.

The reason such risk exists is that, in an efficient market, historical track records—of either securities or money managers—are, by themselves, poor indicators of future performance. Yet it is historical return information that investment management control monitors spin out. No amount of adjustment—for style, for mandate, for risk—can alter the fundamental fact that these returns resemble a close to, if not total, random walk.

Thus, historical performance data—even when supported by information about why returns were what they were—can only play a supporting role in the investment management control function. The leading role in the process of deciding whether to stay with a hand or to ask for new cards goes again to that most indispensable of management tools: judgment.

FIGURE 8-3 Two Quality Control System Signal-to-Noise Ratios

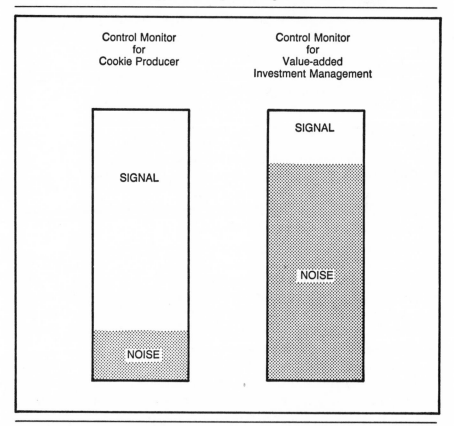

MONITORING PENSION BALANCE SHEET CHANGES AT ALPHA CORPORATION

Within a month after year end, ALPHA's pension asset management team produced an estimated year-end pension system balance sheet. Over the course of the previous year, pension assets at market rose to over $1.5 billion from $1.3 billion at the start. The estimated minimum dollar requirement rose to over $1.0 billion from $0.9 billion. As a result, the asset cushion value went to about $0.5 billion from $0.4 billion. Good news for the shareholders of ALPHA Corporation!

The management pension committee was anxious to learn the causes of the good news. While they were pleased, they were also taken aback by the news. A $100 million increase in the pension plan asset cushion would far outstrip ALPHA's increase in earnings from its regu-

FIGURE 8-4 Pension Balance Sheet Variance Analysis

Asset Value Changes		Liability Value Changes	
Impact of: ($ millions)		Impact of: ($ millions)	
Contributions	$ 15	Normal factors	$ 60
Risk-free return	$130	Special factors	$ 80
Asset mix policy	$100	(change in economic best	
Investment		estimates, $50; change in	
operations	$ 4	benefit promises, $30)	
Total	$249	Total	$140

Asset Cushion Value Change	
Asset value change	$249
Liability value change	$140
	$109

lar operations! The balance sheet variance analysis provided them with the sources of the gain (see Figure 8-4).

In their commentary, the pension asset management team summarized the story behind the numbers in point form. It is reproduced as Table 8-1.

In concluding the balance sheet presentation to the Management Pension Committee, the VP-pension asset management made one final point. As plan liabilities grew 15 percent last year, a $60 million increase in asset cushion would have left the plan's debt/equity ratio unchanged. The asset cushion increase was $49 million more at $109 million.

No immediate decision should be taken on the possible disposition of the $49 million of asset cushion excess (worth $1.53 per share before tax) produced by the fund last year. A year had now passed since ALPHA had reviewed its pension plan asset cushion and asset mix policies. The continued appropriateness of these policies should now be affirmed—or, alternatively, changed in light of today's circumstances.

Putting the Spotlight on Asset Management

The pension balance sheet analysis is ideal for control at the policy level—the responsibility of the management pension committee. Control at the pension asset management level calls for a more disaggregated management information system. Specifically, it should be capable of identifying the sources of value-added (and lost) in the investment management program.

TABLE 8-1 Commentary on Balance Sheet Variance Analysis

Asset-Related

1. Net contributions (gross contributions less benefit payments) added $15 million to plan assets.
2. The minimum risk policy (taken to be 100 percent T-bills here) would have earned 10 percent last year, which would have translated into a $130 million addition to fund value.
3. The capital markets paid for the acceptance of interest rate and equity risk last year. The fund's exposure to these factors produced an incremental 7.7 percent return for the fund, or $100 million.
4. Investment operations added 0.3 percent to fund return, or $4 million.

Liability-Related

1. If last year's economic assumptions had been used this year and no inflation update had been made to pensions-in-pay, liability growth would have been about 7 percent or $60 million.
2. However, the current interest rate structure is about 100 basis points below last year's. This adds about 25 million each to the plan liability to inactive (mainly retired) plan members, and to active plan members.[5]
3. An ad hoc inflation update to pensions-in-pay translates into a $30 million addition to best estimate liabilities.

Asset Cushion Value Change

1. In summary, the risk-free return last year was high enough to produce an asset value increase equal to the plan liability increase. Thus, the asset value increases from investment operations and especially asset mix policy flow through to the bottom line of the pension system. A $109 million increase in asset cushion results.

The key to doing this is to answer an awkward-sounding but important question: What would we have done with this money if we hadn't done what we did? In other words, what was a reasonable alternative to what was actually done? In the case of allocating money to the value-added management style, the reasonable alternative is to put the money into the capital markets passively.

Thus, the benchmark for measuring if a value-added program is indeed adding value, is a well-defined, realistic, implementable passive investment program. Ideally, the benchmark return is adjusted for the estimated cost of actually implementing and managing such a program. If investment in different sectors of the capital markets is contemplated, a series of benchmarks—each meeting the realism criteria—are needed.

Such benchmarks serve another important purpose. When weighted at the asset mix policy weights, they can isolate the impact of a specific policy asset mix on total fund return. So they also play an important role in performing the pension balance sheet variance analysis.

TABLE 8-2 Pension Asset Management Return Monitor

Total Fund

	Last Year
Risk-free return	10.0%
Return increment due to asset mix policy	7.7%
Return increment due to investment operations	0.3%
Total fund return	18.0%
Price inflation	5.5%
Total fund real return	12.5%

External Fund Performance

First quartile break fund	17.2%
Median fund	15.0%
Third quartile break performance	12.8%

Investment Operations Return Increment (policy weights in brackets)

	Component Return	Benchmark Return	Value-Added	Value-Added (weighted)
Domestic stocks (10%)	15.1%	14.1%	1.0%	0.1%
Real estate (10%)	12.3%	12.3%	0	0
Small business (2%)	18.0%	18.0%	0	0
Foreign securities (15%)	15.8%	15.8%	0	0
Zero-coupon bonds (15%)	29.9%	29.9%	0	0
Shift account (10%)	18.1%	17.1%	1.0%	0.1%
The old managers (38%)	16.5%	16.2%	0.3%	0.1%
Net fund value-added				0.3%

ALPHA's pension asset management team identified such benchmarks for each component of the investment program. With the benchmark returns and the actual component returns calculated, they produced the pension asset management report for their first year of operation. Table 8–2 summarizes the results.

The summary is split into three sections. At the total fund level, fund return is decomposed into a risk-free component, an asset mix policy-related component, and a value-added management component. In order to bring an external perspective on the results, the second report section summarizes pension fund return experience in general. The third section decomposes they value-added return into its various sources.

The value-added returns for the real estate and small business programs are set to zero because no usable information suggesting a better (or worse) number is as yet available. The value-added returns in the bond and foreign components are zero because no active programs exist as yet.

The value-added return for domestic stocks is based on the in-place, five-manager program, with each manager having a make money mandate described in the implementation chapter—Chapter Six. The value-added return for the asset mix shift account is based on a two-manager program, with both managers having mandates to aggressively shift money between the stock, bond, and cash markets.

With the implementation of the new investment program proceeding at an orderly pace, 38 percent of the fund was still with the old managers.

From Information to Judgment

The pension asset return monitor (Table 8-2) was produced by the pension asset management team's own microcomputer. Outside data came from the master trustee system and from an independent performance measurement service with a large pension fund data base. Table 8-2 presents the aggregated version of the monitor. More detailed versions showing the performance of individual managers as well as the attribution of the performance are also available to the pension asset management group.

A good start on the internal management information system had been made. But such systems are in a continuous state of evolution, and their development is a science unto itself. But it is not just a science. In building the internal system, the pension asset management team had been surprised at the number of guesses and approximations they had to make along the way.[6]

However, such guesses and approximations cannot throw in doubt the basic theme of last year's investment story. Against the long-term 4 ½ percent real return goal, the fund earned 12 ½ percent. But this extraordinary result came about not through any brilliant moves—either on the part of ALPHA or its investment managers. The very high risk-free real return realized (4 ½ percent) is nothing more than a, likely temporary, gift from borrowers to all lenders.

The 7.7 percent return increment due to asset mix policy was not realized because ALPHA management guessed last year would be a banner year for stocks and especially long bonds. ALPHA's exposure to these asset classes resulted from formally balancing long-term gain prospects against shorter-term pain prospects. This was the asset mix policy decision process we observed in Chapter Four.

Only in the value-added investment components did the scope for making brilliant moves exist. Out of the 4 ½ percent real return goal,

½ percent is to come from value-added management. Last year the still-incomplete program produced 0.3 percent after all fees. In the domestic stocks section, three of the five managers beat their benchmark for the year, one tied, and one underperformed. No surprises there.

One of the two shift account managers called the bond market right and did very well. However, the other one avoided bonds in favor of stocks and cash—leading to significant underperformance relative to the 50 percent stocks–50 percent bonds benchmark. Two of the three managers from the previous investment structure outperformed their benchmarks.

There was nothing in these results that gave the Vice President, pension asset management cause for concern. The investment program was operating within the tolerances established. The regular "walking around" routine meant staying in touch with the managers informally but regularly. The search for new talent would continue.

The VP also set out to pursue another goal. There were forces at work that could have a measurable impact on pension asset management in the future. Some of the issues needing study were very specific—possibly leading to a specific ALPHA response. Others were much broader in nature—possibly leading to fundamental changes in the private pension system as a whole.

The final chapter examines these issues.

CHAPTER NOTES

1. Regulations in the United States emanate from the Employee Retirement Income Security Act of 1974 and subsequent Department of Labor rulings. Canada has both federal and provincial pension regulations, with the type of industry and a plan's place of registration determining jurisdiction.

2. Peter Drucker has probably addressed every management issue there is. This quote came from *Towards the Next Economics and Other Essays*, Harper & Row, 1981, p. 161. We will meet him again in the next chapter.

3. There is, of course, no neat formula for revising economic liability valuation assumptions over time. We are speaking of best estimate assumptions here and not the actuarial assumptions used to establish funding targets. Recall our use of the near-term/far-term split of the future in the asset cushion policy chapter (Chapter Four). The near term is the average length (duration) of the inactive plan liabilities—typically in the seven- to eight-year range. If the inactive plan liabilities are not inflation-sensitive, a 100 basis point move in the seven- to eight-year duration discount rate will change the present value of these liabilities by 7 to 8 percent.

   The far term is all relevant time beyond the near term. Active plan liabilities need to be discounted through both the near term and the far term. But in final earnings plans, liabilities are inflation-sensitive up to retirement. Thus, up to this point, if a change in rates is accompanied by a change in wage inflation expectations of the same magnitude and sign, no change in present value will occur. As for the time period beyond the point of retirement, it is a matter of judgment as to what degree interest rate changes today should affect return expectations 10 to 20 years hence and beyond.

For references to a more technical treatment of these matters, please refer back to notes 1 and 2 in Chapter Two.

4. Actual measurement of these components will lead to a fourth dimension, which may be called "error due to compounding and noninstantaneous rebalancing of benchmark returns." Adding rates of return rather than multiplying wealth relatives also introduces some noise into the process.

5. This is a specific application of the more general discussion of note 3 above.

6. The story of performance measurement is generally accepted to have started with the publication of a Bank Administration Institute study in 1968. Titled *Measuring the Investment Performance of Pension Funds for the Purpose of Inter-fund Comparison*, the study set out a set of measurement principles most of which have withstood the test of time. Volumes have since been written on this topic.

   Art Williams devotes six chapters in his book, *Managing Your Investment Manager* (Dow Jones-Irwin, 1980), to performance measurement. Peter Dietz also gives the topic extensive treatment in *Managing Investment Portfolios* (Warren, Gorham & Lamont, 1983). Walter Good's articles titled "Measuring Performance", (*Financial Analysts Journal*, May–June 1983) and "Accountability for Pension Fund Performance" (*Financial Analysts Journal*, January–February 1984) treat the topic in much the same spirit as we do in this chapter.

   Sometimes a bit of ingenuity is required to create a benchmark portfolio that meets the realism criteria. For example, what is a good real estate benchmark portfolio? Frank Russell Company in the United States and Morguard Properties in Canada have done good work in measuring the—admittedly estimated—performance of large real estate portfolios. But they are specific—albeit large—portfolios. Why not blend in the aggregate return of all open-end real estate pools over a minimum dollar size?

   An even larger challenge exists with small business investments. Period-to-period measures here will be at best rough guesses as to what might be happening in the program. As to a relevant benchmark, maybe the closest alternative to a specific small business investment program is a passive small capitalization stock investment program. Returns for such a program can be measured with the standard tools.

PART FIVE

The Future

CHAPTER NINE

The Private Pension System Challenge: Achieving "Legitimacy"

Never have so many people been shooting . . . at the pension industry at one time.

—M. Clowes

The private pension system has been under attack recently by both politicians and the press. Why? There are many possible specific answers depending on the specifics of the attack.

However, none of these specific answers is likely to get to the heart of the matter. The business philosopher Peter Drucker has probably come closest to identifying the private pension system's Achilles' heel: a lack of "legitimacy."

This chapter looks at Drucker's arguments and their implications for private pension plans, their beneficiaries, and the employers sponsoring these plans.

THE PRIVATE PENSION SYSTEM UNDER ATTACK

A recent speech by Michael Clowes, editor of *Pensions & Investment Age*, had the title "Pension Funds under Fire".[1] In it, he listed no less than eight directions from which the shooting was coming. In (admittedly highly subjective) order of importance by Clowes' judgment, they were:

Private pension efficiency. Suggestions by some legislators that the private pension system is not broad and fair enough to justify the current loss of tax revenues to the federal Treasury.

Pension fund performance. Suggestions by some regulators and the press that pension funds are not only not performing in the sense of beating the averages but are actually causing mischief in the capital markets. They cause market instability with their short-term trading orientation. Large commissions are generated in the process to the benefit only of the broker/dealers executing the transactions.

Terminations and asset reversions. Suggestions by some legislators that this practice proves companies have used pension funds as a place to allow assets to accumulate tax-free with no real intention of providing benefits to the employees. A variation on this theme relates to the practice by some corporations of placing treasury stock rather than cash contributions into the plan. Again, questions about the morality of this practice are raised.

The use and abuse of soft dollars. A growing conviction by legislators, regulators, and press, and even the pension industry itself that the soft-dollar payment mechanism has been abused.[2]

Portability and faster vesting. The argument that—since the average employee stays on the job only four years—quicker vesting and more pension portability is needed has strong political appeal and support.

Noneconomic investment considerations. Increasing pressure to achieve social goals, such as low-income housing or political change, through pension fund investment policies.

Faster growing public sector pension funds. Will they follow "normal" investment practices or will they go their own way, possibly driven by noneconomic considerations?

The shift towards defined contribution plans. What impact will this trend have on the shape of the industry? On the asset mix of pension funds?

Clowes eloquently defended the private pension system against the attacks he considered unfair. The private pension system is indeed doing its job. It is not reasonable to expect it to cover the entire work force. The fact that it appears to have become overfunded through a combination of good returns and high contribution rates is a sign of success, not failure.

If new information is reflected more quickly in security prices today than in the good old days, so what? Where is the evidence pension fund investing is leading to the mispricing of securities? There is none. Would the critics like to return to the good old; individual-investor-dominated-markets of the 1920s? There is criticism that corporate managers are pressing investment managers for short-term performance and that investment managers are doing the same to corporate managers. Who says such pressure must be succumbed to?

He dealt with some of the other issues raised in his closing remarks to the pension industry audience:

> We can try to provide less opportunity for such criticism by being open and forthright, by being prepared to fully disclose our actions. By excercising great care in the discharge of our responsibilities. By being more demanding of ourselves, and of our suppliers and advisers. By accepting that the private pension system might need further evolution to best achieve its goal of providing retirement income for its members.

We wonder how the great American business philosopher Peter Drucker would have responded had he been in the audience. Our guess is that he would have told Clowes his speech was fine but that the sniping at and encroachments on the private pension system by legislators and regulators would not stop until the private sector had dealt with the system's Achilles' heel: in Drucker's words a lack of "legitimacy."

The "Legitimacy" Issue

Peter Drucker wrote an extraordinary—but we suspect not widely read—little book in 1976 titled *The Unseen Revolution—How Pension Fund Socialism Came to America*.[3] In it, he makes the case that American workers, unbeknown to anyone including themselves, had become the beneficial owners of a good part of corporate America. He projected—quite accurately, as things have turned out—that trusteed funds might well raise their equity interest in American business from 25 percent in 1976 to 50 percent 10 years later.[4]

He also foresaw something else. He expressed concern in the book about the private pension system's ability to withstand governmental pressure on two fronts. One stemmed from the government's need for money, the other from its need to regulate. Withstanding such needs would require strong countervailing forces, emanating from within the private pension system itself.

He saw the development of a sense of proprietorship by plan beneficiaries in pension plan assets as the key to developing such countervailing forces. The major blockage to the development of this needed sense of proprietorship was, in his view, the preponderance of defined benefit plans among the larger plan sponsors. With this type of plan, the focus for the plan beneficiary becomes a postretirement stream of payments in no way tied to the return earned by the pension fund.

Not that he advocated a total defined contribution-variable payments pension scheme. Citing the American national college teachers system, CREF–TIAA, as an example, there was no reason why an employer retirement system could not have both a minimum defined payment component and a variable payment component.[5]

Drucker felt very strongly about creating a tangible connection between pension plan members and the ownership of society's means of production. He further recognized that such broad diffusion of ownership created a virtually complete separation between ownership and control. To reconnect the two, he proposed the creation of boards of trustees whose members would truly represent the interests of the plan beneficiaries.

For him, it was the combination of ownership and responsible governance that would give the private pension system, in his words, "legitimacy." With such legitimacy, he saw the private pension system as a socioeconomic force with tremendous wealth-creating power.

The sharp edge of the force would be the allocation of up to 10 percent of pension funds to small business and new venture investments. He argued such a force would be needed to meet the material needs of an American society certain to physically grow older over the coming decades. Only rising capital productivity could offset the negative effects of a rising dependency ratio that accompanies an aging population.[6]

As evidence that the system was not operating anywhere near this potential, he pointed to its tendency to give prudence a regulatory/legal focus rather than an economic one. As a result, pension fund investment practices ended up being influenced as much by rule-oriented considerations as they were by economic/financial considerations.

Overemphasis on investment safety was a consequence to the detriment of the private pension system's role in the wealth creation process and also to the detriment of the beneficiaries' interests through their exclusion from the sharp edge of the wealth-creation process. Only legitimacy through a sense of ownership by the beneficiaries, accompanied by enlightened governance by fund trustees, would set forces in motion to address this safety bias in pension fund investing.

Only the ownership/goverance formula would control the natural tendencies of governments to move in on the private pension system.

The System 10 Years Later

In response to the Clowes speech, Drucker would no doubt make a telling observation. The millions of ordinary Americans and Canadians covered by private sector defined benefit pension plans today have no more sense of proprietorship in the assets of these plans than they did 10 years ago. The governance issue is still outstanding. And defined benefit plans, with their ambiguity surrounding the ownership of plan assets, continue to dominate as the means by which large employers provide pension benefits.

We have argued in this book that the management of the assets of these defined benefit pension plans must be guided by two simple realities. They are that plan assets are first a contingency fund. But subject to this purpose being achieved, corporate managements are obliged to see how the assets may be used to further other corporate goals. We examined these goals in Chapter Two.

There was the profit center focus—having the pension fund, through the pursuit of a high-return policy, contribute to the cost of sponsoring the plan. There was the emergency financial reserve motive—using the plan asset cushion as source of emergency corporate cash. And combined with these considerations, there was the tax-minimization motive, which recognizes the value of the tax deferral the pension fund offers.

Concern about these considerations should not reflect negatively on corporate managers. After all, corporate managers have a responsibility to their shareholders to maximize the value of the common equity. But what if, more and more, the shareholders are the pension funds themselves? Does this mean the traditional guardian of shareholder rights—the corporate director—is the evolving guardian of pension fund and, through it, plan beneficiary rights?

In other words, does the corporate director's role change when he or she represents the interests of hundreds of pension funds in addition to the interests of individual shareholders? We do not see how this can be so. But if we cannot expect corporate directors to represent the interests of trusteed pension funds of defined benefit employer plans any differently than they would the interests of any other shareholder, who can?

But we have come full circle. We are back to the people who do it now—that is, the public servants who enforce the rules and regulations governing trusteed pension fund investments. They will continue as trustee-surrogates until replaced by true private, arms-length trustees. But such trustees can act in the sole interest of the beneficiaries only if the plan assets belong to the beneficiaries.

So maybe the ultimate issue is the nature of the contract between the employer and the employee. Through the issuance of debt—that is, the promise to pay a defined dollar benefit—the employer gets residual use of the trust fund that results. Such an arrangement naturally enhances management's control over the enterprise.

This is so because, as long as the trust fund serves its primary goal of providing benefit security, management retains residual control over the trust fund—control over its size relative to the liabilities, control over its asset mix policy, and control over its investment operations. In such an arrangement, the beneficiary's link to the plan is no different from that of any other debt holder. Legal recourse to assets only results from a failure by the debtor to pay money owed. If Drucker is right about the importance of pension system ligitimacy through some combination of direct ownership by plan beneficiaries and third-party governance, Clowes' last observation in his speech—of a measurable swing to defined contribution plans—is a hopeful sign.

Ownership of assets in this type of plan is unambigious: they legally belong to the beneficiary. As to governance, it is something the employer can now look after in a totally objective, dispassionate fashion. This is so because plan assets can now no longer be used by the employer to achieve any corporate goals.

This purer form of privatization of pension plans, together with enhanced opportunities for personal retirement savings (recommended recently by a Canadian parliamentary study group and proposed in the May 1985 Budget),[7] finally might be moving the system in the direction of greater legitimacy. In the process, individuals are encouraged to become more self-reliant and more involved with planning for the later years in their lives.

Meanwhile, the $1 trillion U.S. pool and $100 billion Canadian pool of assets backing defined benefit employer pension plan liabilities is not likely to just disappear. Nor is its vulnerability to government intervention likely to lessen. Increased governmental control over defined benefit employer pension plans, whatever form it takes, makes politicians winners. Because with such control comes the power to transfer wealth arbitrarily.

There would be two losers. Obviously, the industry built around the private retirement system and the people in it would lose. The number of unemployed stock brokers, money managers, actuaries, and pension consultants would undoubtedly rise. That would be a minor tragedy.

The beneficiaries of employer pension plans would also lose. Today, they have enforceable financial contracts with their employers backed by sufficient assets—specifically segregated for this purpose—to make good their claims. They have a form of property. The more government involvement in the system, the weaker the link between retirement benefits and enforceable contracts backed by segregated assets is likely to become.

Taking such a process to its limits, the beneficiaries lose their property to "society" in return for a governmental promise that "society" will look after them in their old age. That would be a major tragedy.

Pension Reform at ALPHA Corporation

Reflecting on Drucker's book and Clowes' speech, ALPHA's Vice President, pension asset management realized both were valuable study documents for the new company compensation policy task force. With a philosophy and mechanisms in place to address the financial management of ALPHA's current retirement system, senior management wanted to move on and address the system's adequacy for tomorrow.

Specifically, they wanted to examine the whole question of dollars today versus dollars tomorrow in employee compensation. And with respect to the tomorrow dollars, what kind of employer-employee contract best suited the needs of both parties? Was the current contract best? That is, a length-of-service and level-of-pay-related retirement payment promise with a "maybe" on inflation updates? Or should the size of pensions be investment performance-related?

The VP intended to raise the question, "why not both?" with the task force; that is, keep the defined benefit system but add a money purchase component. The master trustee had indicated there would be no difficulty in permitting individuals to tap into ALPHA's pension investment program. Recordkeeping capabilities at the individual level would keep track of the number of units owned and their value. ALPHA's defined benefit plan would simply become one—although very large— participant among many in the pension investment program.

The program could be made available to ALPHA employees for their personal retirement savings. The VP would also be urging study of how the ALPHA retirement system could be made a hybrid defined benefit–defined contribution system. Such a retirement system would appear to offer the best of both worlds.[8] Sure, it would require a more sophisticated approach to retirement planning than most ALPHA employees currently seemed to be taking. But it would seem the employer could be a catalyst in this at very little cost.

These ideas seemed to point in the direction of pension reform at ALPHA which would be in the mutual interest of the employer and the employee. It involved no appeal of any kind for governmental intervention. It involved no increase in pension cost. But it would create a more direct connection between pension plan members and the wealth-creation side of ALPHA's pension system.

And strengthening that connection, reflected ALPHA's pension asset manager, is sorely needed if the private pension system is to remain private.

CHAPTER NOTES

1. The speech was delivered on February 28, 1985, at the Contemporary Hotel, Orlando, Florida, to an investment conference sponsored by the Financial Analysts Federation. Our thanks to Michael Clowes for typing up his speech notes and making them available to us.

2. Soft dollars are an anomaly left over from the old, fixed stock brokerage commission days. Research services were bundled into a total service package provided by the broker. The fee for these research services was included in the fixed-rate schedule. When negotiated commissions replaced the fixed-rate schedule, the old concept of providing a basket of services for one bundled fee did not die. Thus, even today, a payment can be triggered by a money manager which can buy a basket of services.

   The trigger is a buy or sell order placed with a broker. In settling on the fee for performing the transaction, the money manager and the broker discuss two things. One is the dollar amount of the fee. The other is what that dollar amount buys in addition to physically executing the transaction. In the standard case, it is simply access to the broker's research department. However, there are many exceptions to the standard case taking place. Some of these exceptions—if the anecdotes and hearsay are true—would be difficult to square with the fiduciary responsibilities of the transacting parties.

   Quite apart from the alleged abuses of the soft dollar mechanism—the trips, the office equipment, the office rent, etc.—there is another issue. Even in the standard case, money managers are using pension fund money to acquire a service—broker research—which the pension fund itself does not use directly. Should the management fee charged by the money manager not be all inclusive? In other words, should third-party research not be paid for by the money manager rather than by the pension fund?

3. The *Unseen Revolution-How Pension Fund Socialism Came to America*, by Peter F. Drucker, Harper & Row, 1976. An earlier treatise on the social implications of the rise of employer pension plans was published by the Twentieth Century Fund in 1959. It was titled *Pension Funds and Economic Power* and was written by Paul Harbrecht, S.J.

4. The U.S. percentage is probably around 40 percent. The percentage in Canada is lower because almost half of corporate Canada is closely held by powerful Canadian holding companies and by foreign companies. Canadian pension funds do hold about 50 percent of the widely held component of Canadian common shares.

5. The Teachers Insurance and Annuity Association was founded in the 1920s by the Carnegie Foundation. It offers its members a number of annuity options with a minimum floor and payment streams that can range from flat to rising over time. A separate participating equity fund—College Retirement Equities Fund—was started after World War II. Participants were given the option of directing up to 50 percent of their employer's contributions into this equity fund. College professors have used

this option extensively over the years, with the favorite allocation split 50-50 between equities and fixed income. This continued even after up to 100% in equities was allowed.

6. In the United States there is currently one person beyond working age for every three workers. Demographers project this ratio will rise to one in two in 20 or 30 years. The dependency ratio is marginally lower in Canada but will also rise dramatically.

7. Individually-owned pension savings are to be boosted in two ways. First, tax-deductible contribution ceilings into registered retirement savings plans and money-purchase employer plans are to be raised over a number of years. Second, a "locked-in" version of the RRSP is to be created for members of employer pension plans. A major role for this version is to act as depository for the dollar value-equivalent of the vested benefits of a departing or terminated defined benefit plan member.

8. There is no reason why a defined benefit system could not happily coexist beside a money purchase plan. Technically the keys are a good administrative/accounting system and an algorithm that will turn dollars today into dollars tomorrow, and vice versa. With unitized accounting, both the defined benefit plan and the money purchase plan can tap into a single asset management program.

   The other key is to help plan members develop a financial plan for their retirement. This need not be very complicated. Simple guidelines relating equity exposure to years to retirement would go a long way. Ceilings might reach up to 100 percent until age 35 and then decline gradually over the years. Possibly by age 55, equity exposure reaches zero in the money purchase component of the plan, and its assets start to be converted into shorter-term debt securities or annuities.